ASK A LAWYER

DIVORCE AND CHILD CUSTODY

Steven D. Strauss

W · W · NORTON & COMPANY

NEW YORK   LONDON

For information about permission to reproduce selections from this book,
write to: Permissions, W. W. Norton & Company, Inc., 500 Fifth Avenue,
New York, NY 10110.

The text of this book is composed in Berkeley Book, with the display set in
Futura. Desktop composition by Chelsea Dippel. Manufacturing by the Haddon
Craftsmen, Inc. Book design by Margaret Wagner.

Library of Congress Cataloging-in-Publication Data

Strauss, Steven D., 1958–
    Ask a lawyer. Divorce and child custody / Steven D. Strauss.
        p.   cm.
    Includes index.
    ISBN 0-393-04584-6. — ISBN 0-393-31729-3 (pbk.)
    1. Divorce—Law and legislation—United States—Popular works. 2. Custody
of children—United States—Popular works. I. Title.
KF535.Z9S77 1998
346.7301'66—dc21   97-30136
                                                                CIP

W. W. Norton & Company, Inc. 500 Fifth Avenue, New York, N.Y. 10110
http://www.wwnorton.com

W. W. Norton & Company Ltd., 10 Coptic Street, London WC1A 1PU

1 2 3 4 5 6 7 8 9 0

This book is dedicated to my wonderful wife, Maria.
I hope she will never need to use it.

My heartfelt thanks to Michael Stanfield for everything
he has done.

CONTENTS

INTRODUCTION: ABOUT THIS BOOK AND THE *ASK A LAWYER* SERIES

A person usually needs an attorney either to act as an advocate or to get advice. While there are many books on the market that endeavor to teach people how to be their own lawyer-advocate, this is not one of them. This book, and the *Ask a Lawyer* series, focuses upon the second function of an attorney—dispensing helpful, useful, and needed legal advice.

Few can afford to pay $250 to sit down with an attorney for an hour in order to get legal help. The *Ask a Lawyer* series is designed to give people the advice of an attorney at a fraction of the cost. Helping people understand the law and their rights; explaining which of several options may work best for them; giving insights, tips, and helpful hints; in short, giving readers the type of assistance that they would expect if they sat down with an expensive lawyer, *is* the purpose of this book and this series.

Working through a divorce in particular is an area of the law that requires good legal help. As this book explains, there are many facets to the divorce process, and many with important long-term ramifications. This book will help you figure out how to handle your divorce successfully and economically. What is the difference between physical and legal custody? Do you have a right to receive alimony? How should you divide your marital assets? Read on.

This book will sensibly walk you through the divorce process, caution you about possible pitfalls, explain in simple terms important aspects of the process, and guide you toward a resolution that fits your needs. It is organized to make this often complicated area of the law quite easy to understand. Each chapter has its own table of contents, so that once you turn to a chapter of interest to you, you can quickly find the specific area with which you need help. If, for example, you have a question about enforcing visitation rights, flip to Chapter 26, "Violation and Modification," and look under "Interference with visitation or custody." Each chapter ends with "The Important Legal Concept to Remember" so that you leave the topic understanding exactly what it is you need to know.

Appendix A lists many common questions that often arise in the divorce process, along with sensible, simple answers. Any **boldfaced** word in this book can be found in the glossary, Appendix B.

No book of this type can come with a guarantee, and no book can substitute for the advice of an attorney familiar with your particular problems and issues. Nevertheless, this book can easily save you thousands of dollars in how your divorce is handled. Absent many hours with high-priced legal cousel, this book is just about the next best thing.

BEFORE THE DIVORCE

CONTEMPLATING A DIVORCE

Knowing what to expect and making good decisions
The effect of those decisions

KNOWING WHAT TO EXPECT AND MAKING GOOD DECISIONS. The decision to get **divorced** is undoubtedly painful and difficult. Any divorce, even a so-called "simple" one, is usually a messy, emotional, upsetting affair. Aside from the obvious physical impact a divorce will have (for example, you will no longer be living with your spouse, and your children will be going back and forth between two homes), the financial aspect of your divorce will likely be equally disruptive (you will be going from a two-income family to a single-income household, and you may end up renting, not owning a home).

Yet divorce need not be a trauma. There are ways to navigate a divorce sanely, or at least with a degree of sanity, so that you end up comparatively unscathed, in sound financial health, and ready to begin life anew.

The key to that success is twofold. First, *know what to expect*. Understanding the divorce process, knowing the law, knowing what to expect, and having good advice can go a long way to resolving the issues that arise during divorce successfully. Second, *try to make informed, logical decisions*. All too often people allow the emotions experienced during their divorce to poison their judgment. When that happens, they end up making poor decisions, which lead to poor results.

This is not to say that your divorce will be without pain; it will not. However, the key to a successful divorce is to manage that pain in such a way that it does not cloud your judgment. Be as angry and hurt as you need to be, but try your best not to allow your emotions to control your decisions.

THE EFFECT OF THOSE DECISIONS. Good judgment is critical right now. Your emotional and financial future depends upon the quality of the decisions you will make in the next few months. This will likely include decisions regarding whether to keep a house or to sell it, figuring out where the kids will live, deciding what debts to take on and which to give to your spouse, and determining whether to fight or cooperate with your soon-to-be ex-spouse. Any one of these decisions may have critical long-term ramifications that you presently probably do not even realize. For example:

> Susie was fed up with her husband of ten years and wanted out of the marriage, no matter what the cost. She moved out and filed for divorce. Her husband, Spencer, represented himself in the proceedings. Susie's attorney drafted a marriage settlement agreement that Spencer agreed to. The agreement gave Susie sole physical custody of their three-year-old daughter, Jillian, and she was to share legal custody with Spencer. She did not know the difference between physical and legal custody, and she didn't really care, for that matter. She just wanted out. Ten years later, Susie fell in love again and wanted to move to another state to be with her new fiancé. Because she had sole physical custody of Jillian, Spencer had a difficult time stopping her.

So this is your word of caution: the decisions you make today will be affecting your life for many years to come. Understand this process. Know your rights and responsibilities. Think long-term. Be aggressive yet compassionate. But, above all, be sane and informed. You, and your children, deserve no less.

The Important Legal Concept to Remember: Divorce can be confusing if you do not know the process. Knowing what to expect can help you make good decisions.

2

STEPS IN A DIVORCE (HOW LONG WILL THIS TAKE?)

The steps in a divorce case
How the case may end
Settlement versus trial

THE STEPS IN A DIVORCE CASE. A divorce begins when one spouse files a **petition,** or a **complaint,** against the other. A complaint is just what it sounds like: one person is complaining, in legal language, about what the other person did. It identifies the **parties,** states the reasons for the divorce, and requests relief from the court. After the complaint is filed (by the party called either the **plaintiff** or the **petitioner**) it is sent, along with the **summons,** to the other party. This is called **serving** them. Typically, the person being sued (named as either the **defendant** or the **respondent**) has thirty days to file a **response** with the court and the other side. Once the response is filed, the lawsuit has officially begun.

The next phase of the divorce process is spent conducting **discovery.** Discovery is the formal process that allows both sides to discover information from the other. How much property does he actually own? How much is her retirement plan worth? Once this information is exchanged, the parties are in

a place where realistic divis
end is in sight.

The filing of the complai
covery process, can take as s
a few years. It depends upo
complexity of the issues, and
As a general rule, the more m
will take. And if, besides mo
children and/or anger, then
about; you could be in for a v
divorce. Conversely, if you ha
then there should be no reason
quick, inexpensive, simple matter.

depends upon the a
a lot of assets to
trial. It is far b
and your
ble and
one

HOW THE CASE MAY END. Like any lawsuit, a divorce case
can end in one of five ways:

1. The parties agree to a settlement.
2. The parties cannot agree on anything and the case goes to trial.
3. The parties agree to a partial settlement and save the unresolved issues for trial.
4. Either the petitioner or the court dismisses the case (the respondent cannot dismiss a case).
5. The respondent fails to answer the complaint and loses by **default**.

Of those five possibilities, the third, fourth, and fifth are
relatively rare. Partial settlements occasionally occur. Dismissal
occurs in divorce only when the petitioner changes his mind
and drops the case. Default occurs when the other side is too
lazy or ignorant to respond.

The first possibility, settlement, is the best option in most
divorce cases. In fact, 95 percent of all civil cases (meaning all
cases, not just divorce) settle out of court. Again, much

itudes of the parties. Just because there are
divide, the case need not turn ugly and go to
etter for everyone concerned—you, your spouse,
hildren—if the adults act as civil and fair as possi-
try to reach a settlement. Not only will this save every-
much grief, and a lot of attorneys' fees, but it also will like-
y ensure a better result for you.

SETTLEMENT VERSUS TRIAL. Consider the two tacks a case can take. Either it can settle or it can go to trial. When a party decides it wants to win at all costs, it will opt against settlement. This is called litigating a case. Do not be naïve. **Litigation** is war. When you decide to litigate a case to the end, it means you are willing to risk all or nothing at trial. It also means being as adversarial as possible in order to win.

The advantage of this tactic is twofold. Because trial is basically a win-lose proposition, it first means you may get everything you want. It also is sure to anger your spouse and cost him a lot of money. That too may be just what you want.

Yet trial is an inherently dangerous proposition. The problem is that when you litigate toward trial, you must proceed under the assumption that the judge will decide the case in your favor. Because that is a dangerous premise, the downside of going to trial usually far outweighs any advantages.

The problem is that judges, by nature and law, do not take sides. Their job is to be independent, fair, objective, intelligent, rational, and law-abiding. While you may be positive that you will win, in the judge's mind your chances are, at best, fifty-fifty. You can also rest assured that if you take your divorce to trial, your spouse will be just as willing as you to say and do almost anything in order to win. He or she will be vigorously represented. The judge may believe you, or he may believe your mate. Favorable evidence may be allowed in, or it may not. The old legal saying, learned the hard way by many a litigant, is "You never know what a judge or a jury will do."

This cannot be emphasized enough. Some judges are brilliant, some are not. Some are sympathetic, some are cold. It is a complete roll of the dice to put your fate in the hands of a judge. By taking a case to trial, you are allowing a person who is unfamiliar with you, your children, and your situation to decide your fate. In the end, it will be this third party who hardly knows you who will finally decide who gets what and where your kids will live. The result could easily be terrible.

Because of that distinct possibility, it is almost always in everyone's best interest to settle the case rather than try it. Settlements ensure that it is you and not a third party who decides your fate. Between you, your spouse, and your attorneys, a fair and equitable result for all concerned can be achieved. While you may not get everything you want, you are far more likely to get more of what you want through settlement than through trial. Settling has the added advantage of usually ensuring that the case will be resolved far more quickly and much less expensively than it would if it goes to trial.

The moral is that the length of your divorce is in your hands. Generally speaking, if you and your spouse can work out a fair property division and an acceptable child custody/visitation arrangement, then there is no reason that it should take more than, say, nine months to get divorced, from start to finish. On the other hand, again in general, if you cannot work things out, and you end up at trial, your divorce could easily take two years.

The Important Legal Concept to Remember: Everyone wants to "win" their case, yet neither side ever wins in a divorce. Property is split, debts are divided, custody is determined. It is almost always better if you decide these things for yourself rather than allowing a judge to decide them for you. You never know what a judge will do.

3

ON HIRING AND WORKING WITH A LAWYER

Do you need a lawyer?
Finding a good attorney
The initial meeting
What to look for
How to know if your attorney is doing a good job

DO YOU NEED A LAWYER? The very first question to ask is whether a lawyer is even necessary in your case. The answer is usually yes, but not always. More than anything, it depends on the complexity of the case. A couple who has been married a short time (under three years), without a lot of property, and without children can probably get divorced without the aid of attorneys. Because most divorces are spent dividing property, debts, and time with children, marriages without those things are usually relatively simple affairs.

Conversely, a marriage of some length usually does involve property, children, or both. In that case, hiring an attorney is advisable. These matters are usually both too emotional and too complicated for a nonlawyer to handle.

Marty was an intelligent man who owned his own business and decided to represent himself in his divorce. His wife,

Sandy, hired an attorney to help her through the ordeal. At their first hearing before the judge, Sandy's attorney made Marty look quite foolish. At the end of the hearing the judge ruled in Sandy's favor. He then peered down over his bench and asked Marty: "Sir, I have one question for you, do you perform surgery on yourself as well?"

Even attorneys rarely represent themselves. There is an old saying in the law: "The lawyer who represents himself has a fool for a client." The reason that neither attorney nor layman should represent himself in his divorce is that an attorney's job is threefold, and the three functions cannot simultaneously be done properly by a person who is both attorney and client. First, because he or she is not a party to the case, an attorney acts as an impartial arbiter; a good attorney will tell you the strengths and weaknesses of your case. Those individuals who act as their own attorney often are too caught up in their side of the facts to see the problems in their case. Second, the attorney is an expert. She has gone through four years of college, three years of law school, and many years of practice. She knows far more about divorces and divorce law than any layman. Finally, an attorney is an advocate; her job is to represent her client zealously. Although you may be able to perform this third function adequately, you would still be unable to perform the other two functions properly. Do not be mistaken: if you do represent yourself in your divorce, you too would likely have a fool for a client.

FINDING A GOOD ATTORNEY. The best place to find a good attorney is from a satisfied customer. Word-of-mouth advertising will tell you far more about a lawyer than a dozen television commercials. If you know someone who has been through a divorce recently, find out how she liked her lawyer. What kind of result did she get? Ask whether the lawyer returned phone calls promptly and how much money she spent.

Similarly, if you have a friend who is a lawyer, ask her, but don't hire her. There are more good lawyers than good friends around. Not only will you need to confess many intimate secrets to your attorney (who, by the way, has an obligation to keep them secret), but by the end of your case you may not like your lawyer very much (having possibly spent a lot of money on results you find unsatisfactory). It is far better just to ask your lawyer-friend's opinion about whom to hire than to hire her.

If you do not know any attorneys, and do not know anyone who knows any, then it gets a bit more difficult. Try to stay away from any referral services other than those sponsored by your local **bar association**. Other referral services, found in the Yellow Pages, usually have but one requirement of the attorneys they recommend—money. Any lawyer who pays the fee required by the referral service will probably be recommended by that service. The local bar association is an organization of local lawyers grouped by practice area who often have a referral service based on expertise, not profit.

Also, most libraries have a set of books called the *Martindale-Hubble Law Directory*. These books list attorneys by state and city; each listing indicates what areas the particular firm practices in, and each firm lists the experience of each attorney working there.

The final option is advertising. Almost all attorneys, good and bad alike, now advertise. If a Yellow Page or television ad catches your fancy, and the attorney practices in divorce, schedule an interview and go speak with her.

THE INITIAL MEETING. After you have found one or more attorneys whom you might like to hire, schedule an initial meeting to interview them. This meeting should be free. Most attorneys rarely charge when meeting with a new client for the first time. Remember this: the attorney needs you more than you need her. Competition among lawyers is fierce. The purpose of the meeting is to see if you want this particular lawyer, not to see if she wants you. By the time your case is over, you will have paid your attorney a good amount of money. You should feel comfortable with her. While shopping for an attorney, keep in mind that many people getting divorced find that they like having an attorney of the same sex.

Make sure to ask the following questions at the first meeting with a lawyer:

- Will she be your attorney, or will she assign your case to a **paralegal** or a young **associate**?
- How long has she been in practice?
- Does she specialize in divorce?
- Does she believe in trying or settling cases?
- What does she charge per hour, and how much of a **retainer** does she require?
- Would she be willing to do the case for a **flat fee**?
- What kind of result should you expect to see in your case, and how much will it likely cost you?
- What are the best and worst case scenarios for your case?
- How long should your case take?
- Does she have any references (former clients) with whom you can speak?

WHAT TO LOOK FOR. Good attorneys are honest, hard-working, and committed. They return phone calls promptly, tell you the truth, and are smart. Because so many difficult choices lay ahead, above all you need someone whose judgment you trust. While this is obviously difficult to gauge in one meeting, make sure that you feel comfortable with the lawyer and that you seem to have a good rapport with her.

You want someone who specializes in divorce, and someone who will give you courteous, personal, prompt attention. Law firms of ten attorneys or more tend to be more impersonal than smaller firms, and they may not be any better. In divorce cases especially, a smaller firm that concentrates on divorce, or a **solo practitioner**, is likely to give you the kind of attention that you want, deserve, and will be paying for.

HOW TO KNOW IF YOUR ATTORNEY IS DOING A GOOD JOB.
You will get a bill that may shock you from your attorney every
month. Lawyers often spend time on tasks the client never sees,
but which must be done: dealing with opposing counsel over
the phone, responding to and writing letters, legal research,
etc. How do you know if your money is being well spent?

There is one true barometer of an attorney's competence:
results, large and small alike. Large results are things like winning motions and arbitrations, and getting the property or custody arrangement that you want. Small results are things like
answering phone calls within twenty-four hours, meeting with
you on short notice when need be, or offering solutions to end
the case more quickly and cheaply.

Besides the competence of your counsel, results in your
divorce also depend on the facts of the case. For example, a
husband who walks out on his wife and children of fifteen
years, who fails to pay temporary child support, who makes
far more than his wife, and who has a history of abuse should
not expect a favorable result in his case, no matter how good
his lawyer is. That is a husband with bad facts. In contrast, a
husband who has been supportive, who earns an amount similar to his wife, and who has cared for the children since birth
should expect a good result, no matter how awful his attorney.
That husband has good facts. If you have bad facts, do not
expect a good result.

**The Important Legal Concept to Remember: Not all attor-
neys are alike in personality or ability. Interview a few spe-
cialists, and hire the one you are most comfortable with.
With good facts, expect good results.**

WHAT YOU SHOULD EXPECT TO PAY

Attorneys' fees

Keeping costs down

Compare the following scenarios:

> Bruce and Gwen were married for twenty-three years before they called it quits. Although they both agreed that divorce was in their best interests, they had accumulated a lot of assets in their many years together. So, even though their divorce was amicable, it was still time-consuming, and, accordingly, expensive. By the time all was said and done, each of them had spent in excess of $10,000 on their respective lawyers.

> Donna and Jim were married only five years, and the only thing they had to show for their marriage was their beautiful daughter, Anne. The main issue in their case, custody, was easily resolved when they agreed that Anne should continue to live with Donna. Their divorce cost less than $3,000, total.

ATTORNEYS' FEES. The cost of divorce depends on two factors—issues and attitudes. Issues are all the things that must be decided before the divorce is final: child custody, division of assets and debts, alimony, and child support. The more issues involved, the more the case will cost. Couples with few assets and no children have few issues. That divorce should be inexpensive.

Whereas issues are generally beyond your control (either you have them or you do not), attitudes *are* in your control. You can decide to make your spouse's life hell during the divorce, or not. You can drag him into court every few months, or decide not to. You can choose to pay or ignore temporary child and spousal support. Anger is understandable during divorce, but it comes with a price. The more difficult you are (or your spouse is) the more your divorce will cost.

As stated previously, simple, **uncontested divorces** can, and probably should, be done without the assistance of lawyers. Books with preprinted legal forms are available, as are paralegals. A paralegal *is not* an attorney, and cannot give legal advice. What he can do is help prepare the paperwork. A simple, amicable divorce done without the aid of counsel should generally cost no more than $500.

Contested divorces litigated through lawyers can cost anywhere from $500 to $50,000 or more, depending upon the issues and attitudes involved. Divorce lawyers usually charge anywhere from $100 to $500 per hour, based on their locale and ability. They do not take cases on **contingency**. As in much of life, you often get what you pay for. Cheaper lawyers are probably less experienced and less qualified than their higher priced counterparts. They also often charge clients for more time than the case actually takes in order to recoup the lower fee. This is not to say that you need to hire a high-priced legal eagle; rather, it is a word of caution to do your homework and find the best lawyer available at a price you can afford.

But be forewarned: *legal help is expensive.* When you combine student loans, rent, payroll, malpractice insurance, ego, and greed, there is no way around it. Attorneys are paid to do things that laypeople cannot do themselves. Just because you can use a knife does not mean you can also take out your own gallbladder. So too just because you can read and write does not mean that you can draft a **brief** and get a judge to rule in your favor.

KEEPING COSTS DOWN. While an hourly wage for an attorney is usually par for the divorce course, if you can negotiate a flat fee, do so. A flat fee is usually acceptable in divorces in which the parties need help resolving just a few issues. It will almost always result in a lower fee, as attorneys who are paid by the hour charge for *every minute* they put into the case: phone calls, letters, etc. There is, accordingly, no incentive to be efficient. Indeed, there is a great incentive to be inefficient. The flat fee forces the attorney to handle the case quickly and economically. It prevents hourly-fee abuses.

Even if you cannot get a flat fee, here are some tips that should help to decrease your legal fee:

- Get your attorney to agree not to charge for phone calls and other tasks that take less than five minutes.
- Get him to charge you his cost, and no more, for copies, faxes, etc. Law firms make a lot of money off the markup on their so-called "expenses"—things like faxes, copies, etc. Many charge twenty-five cents a page per copy, and one dollar a page for a fax. If you challenge this fee, it should be reduced.
- Help him. Any legwork that you do is time your attorney does not have to spend on your case. Organizing documents and making lists of assets and debts can help.

The Important Legal Concept to Remember: Good legal help is expensive. By having the right attitude and by negotiating with your attorney, you can help to keep your costs down.

SEPARATION AND DIVORCE

DOMESTIC VIOLENCE

Child abuse
Solutions
Spousal abuse
Solutions

There are many causes for separation and divorce; no two situations are alike. Generally, however, divorce causes can be divided into two categories: **no-fault** reasons, such as irreconcilable differences; and **fault**-oriented reasons, such as adultery and domestic violence. (See Chapter 7, "Divorce: An Overview.") Domestic violence is a fault-oriented reason for divorce.

No one has the right to hit someone else. It is both a crime and a **tort**. That means that if someone hits someone else, not only can he be arrested for the crime but he can also be sued in civil court for money damages as well. Even more important, and often more effective legally, is that a spouse who abuses another, or a parent who abuses a child, will almost always lose the divorce case. He will not be granted custody, may even be denied visitation, will also pay dearly financially, and will probably be arrested.

CHILD ABUSE. Everyone, a child especially, has the right to be free from violence. Child abuse can take many forms, and, again, most of them are both crimes and torts. No parent has the right to raise her child "as she sees fit" if that definition includes abuse. Physical abuse and sexual abuse are illegal, and the perpetrator can go to jail for a very long time.

Physical abuse is that type of behavior which negligently or intentionally causes physical harm to a child, resulting in injury. While an occasional swat on the bottom would not meet this definition, consistent, perpetual swats would. Wrestling with a child is fine; punching and kicking a child is not.

Child abuse can also be emotional in nature, involving actions such as screaming at the child, public humiliation, denigration, and persistent belittlement. **Child neglect** too is a form of abuse. It is the negligent or intentional disregard of the child's needs—failing to feed and clothe the child properly, or leaving the youngster unsupervised for too long, are examples.

Sexual abuse is illegal and punishable by law, and can be committed by any adult against a child, not just the parent. Such behavior involves any inappropriate touching of the child in any manner, and even sexual innuendo. Any type of action toward the child that leads to the sexual pleasure of the adult is considered sexual abuse, even that which is far from intercourse.

SOLUTIONS. There are several solutions available, but the first and best advice is to separate the child from the perpetrator *immediately*. Pending divorce, one can also

1. *Call the police:* The police can help best during a crisis. Although they will not likely arrest the perpetrator upon the first call, they can direct you to appropriate crisis counselors in your community. After a restraining order is obtained (see below) and the abuse or the threat of the abuse happens again, the police will arrest the abuser.

2. *Get a restraining order:* A **TRO** (temporary restraining order) is an emergency order issued by a judge forbidding the abuser from certain actions (for example, from coming within one hundred yards of the child). It may also order the

abusive parent to leave the family home. If the abuser violates the order, call the police immediately, and the person
will be arrested and put in jail. A TRO can usually be
obtained in a day with the help of a lawyer or a women's
shelter.

3. *Call a child protection agency:* Almost every community has a
   social service agency intended to protect children. They will
   investigate the claims made, and if evidence is found to support the allegation of abuse, the child will either be moved
   out or otherwise kept from the abuser. Note, however, that
   once a government social service agency enters the situation,
   you become its "client," and it will be a part of your life for
   some time to come. This may be helpful or horrible.

4. *Call a crisis shelter:* There are many organizations that will
   help. They can be found in the Yellow Pages under "Crisis
   Intervention Services," "Women's Shelters," "Mental Health,"
   "Social Workers," or "Counseling." Good referrals can also
   come from friends, priests and rabbis, doctors, school advis-
   ers, and the local welfare agency.

Child abuse should never be tolerated, and the abuser
deserves whatever legal guns you can point at him.

SPOUSAL ABUSE. Like children, women too have the right to
live in their homes free from violence. When one spouse hits
another, it is a **battery** under the law. Women may be battered
in many ways—again, physically, emotionally, and sexually.

Amazingly, spousal rape is still not considered domestic violence in some states. Rape is legally defined as unconsented
sexual intercourse. When two people are married, according
to these states, the marriage equals consent, and therefore no
crime is committed during unconsented sex.

Battered Women's Syndrome is a recent development in the
law to explain a cycle of violence and reconciliation between a
battered woman and her abusive partner. A typical pattern goes
something like this: the man hits the woman while in a rage,

and then later acts sweet and kind to her in an effort to keep her under his power. The woman hates the violence but loves the compassion. Knowing that he may hurt her worse if she were to leave, and having a depreciated sense of self-esteem, she stays in the abusive relationship. Eventually, the woman may rage back and kill her tormentor.

Although it is increasingly used as a defense when such women are tried for murder, as of yet, Battered Women's Syndrome is rarely successful in court. The reason is that the law allows a person to defend herself against an immediate threat of violence with only *the same amount of force* and no more. If the man hits the woman, she can legally hit him back, but she cannot legally shoot him dead (even though she may want to and have every reason to) because the law deems this an excessive use of force for the threat presented. It is only the immediate threat of death that will allow a woman to kill her perpetrator in self-defense legally.

SOLUTIONS. The solutions available to a woman who is being abused by her mate are much the same as those offered to the spouse whose child is being abused. Call the police, get a restraining order, call a shelter, *get out!*

The most important thing someone can do when being abused is to get away from her abusive mate and file for divorce. The shelter solution is especially helpful. Shelters can offer temporary housing, legal help, and the chance to be safe.

One more solution: call the National Domestic Violence Hotline. This is a confidential hotline that offers crisis counseling, local referrals, and legal help. The number is 1-800-799-7233.

The Important Legal Concept to Remember: Abuse is wrong and should not be tolerated. Many people and organizations are available to assist in the difficult transition from abuse to independence.

SEPARATION

THE RISKS OF SEPARATION. Many couples use a trial separation to test the waters of divorce. It enables them to see whether they want to live without one another, and allows hot tempers to cool and frayed feelings to heal. While not often successful, separation, be it trial or permanent, can at least ease the way toward divorce. What is important to know legally is that some of the decisions made during separation can have important consequences in the divorce, however innocent they may seem at the time.

For example, upon an impending separation, the question often arises as to who will move out of the family home. The primary caretaker of the children usually stays, and the other mate usually moves. While understandable, and even laudable, know that it is a *financial risk* for the one who decides to move. Why? Courts like the **status quo** and are loath to change it; the one who moves often never lives in the house again.

Jerry owned a home for fifteen years before he met Carol and she moved in with him. After being married only nineteen months, Carol asked for a trial separation. Jerry offered to move out in the hopes that he would win Carol back. Ten days later, Carol served him with divorce papers and a TRO that ordered him to stay at least one hundred yards away from her. Jerry could not go home, and Carol was allowed to live in Jerry's house throughout the entire two years of the divorce proceedings.

A decision to move out of state with the children after separation can also be very risky. Needless to say, a husband would probably not approve of such a decision, and, in all likelihood, a judge would agree with him. Unless one parent has proven himself to be unworthy, the law wants both parents to share in the upbringing of the children. And until one parent is awarded **physical custody** of the children, a parent should not make unilateral decisions regarding where the kids will live. Thus, a parent who moves the children away from the other parent interferes with that parent's parental rights. The one who moves may end up losing custody of the kids altogether in the final **divorce decree**.

Dennis and Dana decided to separate after a tumultuous two-year marriage. Dana, happy just to be rid of Dennis, told him that he could have the house and their child, Elizabeth, while she traveled for a while. While she was gone, Dennis proved to be a wonderful father to Elizabeth, and was awarded sole custody upon Dana's return.

SEPARATION AND MONEY. Separation can also have a legal effect on your debts and credit, on your income and property, and on retirement and pension benefits.

1. *Debts and credit:* Debts incurred after the separation are usually the separate debt of the mate who incurred the debt. The problem is that there is quite a bit of time between separation and the final divorce decree. Even though a couple may be separated, both are still *legally liable* for debts incurred on joint accounts until the divorce is final. If one spouse

defaults on a payment while separated, the other will be held responsible. Creditors have the right to come after either spouse for debts created during the marriage unless the couple is legally separated (see below).

In some states the debts created and property bought between separation and divorce are considered separate. To be safe, it is best to assume that while you are separated both assets and debts remain the joint responsibility of both partners.

> Gail and Chris were married for three years. Chris was tired of Gail spending all of his money, so he moved out and filed for divorce. The day after she was served with the divorce papers, Gail ran up a $10,000 bill on their joint credit card. When the divorce was final, the court ordered Chris to pay $5,000 of that bill.

Your credit too can be adversely affected by a separation. While married and still living together, each spouse can keep an eye on the other to make sure that bills are paid on time. Once one partner moves out, there is little preventing the other from not paying certain bills out of revenge.

The best way to protect yourself financially after separating is to go to court immediately and get a **legal separation**. *Just because you are living apart does not mean that you are legally separated.* A finding by the judge that the couple is legally separated results in a court order to that effect. The order states that the couple is separated, and it enunciates the terms of the separation, including payment of particular debts. Thereafter, debts are no longer joint. Court orders that prove you are separated carry much more weight than any letter of explanation to a creditor that you could write.

2. *Income and property*: It is said that possession is nine tenths of the law. Like many clichés, it is mostly true. The property a spouse takes when he moves out will probably be the property he keeps in the final agreement, give or take a few changes. If one spouse takes the rocking chair that the other

loves, there is really little that can be done to get it back, absent obtaining an expensive court order. And even then, the chair might be sold or "lost" in the meantime. *When separating, then, make sure to take what you want with you.*

Income that you earn after separation will likely be considered your separate money, unless you earn it from a joint business that you run with your mate. Investments and property are valued at the time of *divorce*, not separation, and thus any appreciation between the time of separation and divorce will be divided equally.

3. *Pensions and retirement plans*: A spouse is entitled to a share of her partner's employee pension plan earned while married. Unlike other property, retirement valuations are made at the time of *separation*, not divorce. Any increase in a pension plan between the time of separation and divorce, therefore, is not shared.

AVOIDING COMMON MISTAKES. People often leave a marriage in a fit of anger. This can lead to many potential problems—they may lose property, get stuck with unwanted debts, become financially responsible for trips to Hawaii that they didn't take. Many of these problems are fairly easy to avoid with just a little planning and follow-through.

Before moving out, be sure to

· Make copies of all bills and important financial documents;
· Make a videotape of all possessions;
· Identify which items you will want to take with you;
· Apply for credit cards in your own name.

After you move out, be sure to

· Notify all creditors of your new status and new address;
· Immediately close all joint checking accounts. Consider also closing all other joint accounts, including all savings

accounts, deposit accounts, safe deposit boxes, lines of credit, and credit cards. Be careful when closing joint accounts, though—you do not want to steal your mate's money; it may come back to haunt you later in the divorce. Give him his fair share and say good-bye;

· Notify all credit cards of the change and ask them to cancel all joint cards.

SEPARATION AGREEMENTS. Many of the nasty problems arising from a separation can be avoided by working with and not against your spouse if at all possible. Of course this will be difficult. It is also smart. You will clearly save money and usually get a better result from cooperation than from confrontation, however emotionally satisfying the latter might be.

One way to work together is to write up a separation agreement. This agreement can delineate who is responsible for what while the divorce proceedings continue. While the document can be as simple or as complicated as the situation warrants, it probably should cover the following items at a minimum:

· Distribution of debts (who pays what bills)
· Distribution of assets (cars, furniture, etc.)
· A parenting plan (where the children will live, visitation times)
· Child and spousal support payments

The Important Legal Concept to Remember: Even though you are separated, you are still married. Work together if possible, but make sure to protect your interests. The best way to do that is to get a legal separation.

7

DIVORCE: AN OVERVIEW

A SUGGESTED COURSE OF ACTION. The decision to actually go forward with a divorce is not one to be taken lightly. Aside from the obvious emotional turmoil sure to be unleashed comes a flood of new financial problems: attorneys often ask for retainers in the thousands of dollars, deposits for apartments are required, counseling may be needed.

Do not do anything rash. There are few times in life more harried than the first few weeks after deciding to divorce. And this is when mistakes such as becoming violent, hiding children, or selling assets are often made. Such mistakes can have long-term negative consequences.

After becoming situated, the first thing to do is to hire an attorney who will draft and serve the divorce complaint. It makes no difference, though, whether you serve your mate or he serves you. After an answer is filed, the divorce usually proceeds like this: the couple spends several months or years trying to figure out how their assets and/or children can best be divided. Allegations fly back and forth. Children travel back and forth. The couple eventually tires of each other enough to allow for settlement. If they are really stubborn, they foolishly opt for trial. (See Chapter 23, "Trial.")

A better course of action is less adversarial. While you may legitimately be angry at your husband, some things are better left unsaid. And they are left unsaid out of a desire to *get the best possible result*, not out of any misguided sense of altruism. The best deals, be they in business or divorce, are deals in which both parties get most of what they want. A one-sided deal invites the other side to **breach** it. You will find (possibly the hard way) that it is better to try to work with your spouse than to fight over everything. Although fights are inevitable, cooperation in the face of adversity is preferable.

GROUNDS FOR DIVORCE AND ANNULMENT. A divorce is different from an **annulment**. A divorce ends a valid marriage, whereas an annulment means that the marriage was invalid from its inception. Grounds for an annulment include being under age at the time of marriage, bigamy, fraud, duress, and mental incompetence. Annulling a marriage takes an act of court, and a decree of annulment means that the marriage never occurred.

Traditionally, a divorce was granted only if one of the partners was found to be at "fault"—if they did something wrong. This fault-oriented divorce concept was prevalent until the 1970s, and is still available today, albeit less often. Grounds for divorce because of fault include matters such as criminal convictions, nonsupport, adultery, imprisonment, insanity, impotence, violence, and alcoholism.

Every state now has some form of no-fault divorce (although some states are considering revoking no-fault). No-fault means precisely that: neither party needs to prove that the other did anything wrong in order to get a divorce. All the person seeking the divorce has to do is state at the outset of the proceedings that there are irreconcilable differences or that the marriage is irretrievably broken (depending upon the state).

Many states offer both fault and no-fault grounds for divorce, either can be alleged in the complaint, and the decision as to which way to go really depends upon your state laws. The main difference between the two is in the proof required to get the divorce. No-fault requires no proof, and fault requires proof of the fault alleged. If a wife decides to sue on fault grounds alone, she has to be prepared to prove that the husband did something wrong. If she cannot, the divorce could ostensibly be denied, although that is rare. More often fault is alleged in the complaint because the state's laws may grant some benefit to the spouse found not at fault—custody, increased child support, higher alimony, etc.

> Susan and Brian lived in Virginia and were married for twenty-five years when Brian caught Susan cheating on him. Brian sued Susan for divorce on fault grounds and won. Although Susan had been a wonderful wife, she received no spousal support because the law in her state forbade awarding it when the spouse is guilty of adultery.

Other states have similar laws. In some states, an adulterous spouse will likely have a more difficult time getting custody of the kids, and many states permit the court to consider marital misdeeds when dividing property.

DEFENSES TO DIVORCE. There is no defense to a no-fault divorce. If one partner wants one, then there is little the other spouse can do about it. Defenses to divorce are really only applicable in those thirty-five states that continue to allow fault-oriented divorces.

In the case where the petitioner chooses to proceed with a fault-oriented divorce, several defenses are available to bar the divorce and remain married (for whatever reasons one may have). An attorney can explain these defenses and clarify whether they might apply in a particular case.

FOREIGN DIVORCES. Many people, indeed most people, understandably want to get their divorce over with as quickly as possible. Rather than submit to the **jurisdiction** and tedious process involved in their state's legal system, some people opt to try to get divorced in a different state or country that may have a reputation for fast divorce proceedings. Collectively, divorces obtained in different countries or different states are called "foreign divorces."

In order for a divorce in a different *state* to be valid, generally, one of the spouses must be living in the state where the divorce is sought. Both spouses must also agree to the jurisdiction (authority) of that state to grant the divorce. Without both requirements—residency of one spouse and consent of both spouses—a foreign state's divorce will be invalid in the home state. It will have the same legal effect as if no divorce proceedings ever occurred.

Divorces in other *countries* are often also called quickie divorces. They can take place in Mexico, the Dominican Republic, or some other country. They happen much faster there than in the United States—often in a matter of a few days. Unfortunately, quickie divorces are quite risky, as they too are often deemed to be invalid once the couple gets back to the United States. Check with an attorney to see how these divorces are received in your state.

The Important Legal Concept to Remember: Cooperation almost always beats confrontation in today's no-fault world of divorce, although the "fault" of one spouse may affect the outcome of the case. Foreign divorces, while available, usually fail to give the desired result.

PROPERTY

8

MARITAL PROPERTY

Types of property
Community property
Equitable distribution
Taking the risk out of the division process

Divorce courts are far more interested in protecting children and in the financial aspects of a divorce than in the emotional problems between spouses. In fact, the division of property and debts will likely be among the most important *legal* aspects of your divorce. The misdeeds, trysts, and abuses of a spouse, while important as far as fault goes, carry little weight when it comes to dividing the property.

TYPES OF PROPERTY. There are three types of property in a divorce: your separate property, your spouse's separate property, and joint marital property. Classification of property is critical in a divorce since how property is classified largely determines who gets it upon divorce.

Separate property is property owned outright by either spouse. The other spouse has no claim or legal interest in that property, and upon divorce, that property will remain with the mate who owned it.

A week before she was married, Rita bought stock in a new company called Microsoft. The stock was in her name alone, and she owned it for the twenty years she was married. The stock is Rita's alone. Upon divorcing, her husband Victor would have no claim to it.

Whether property is considered separate depends upon individual state laws. The nine community property states are Arizona, California, Idaho, Louisiana, Nevada, New Mexico, Texas, Washington, and Wisconsin. Puerto Rico is also a community property jurisdiction. In the community property states, there are five categories of property that are considered separate:

1. Property owned prior to marriage;
2. Property bought while married using funds that can be traced to ownership prior to marriage;
3. Property acquired by either spouse during marriage through either gift or inheritance;
4. Property owned by the couple that is intentionally, and in writing, given to the other spouse as her sole, separate property;
5. Property acquired after separation.

In the forty-one other states, called **equitable distribution** states, while these five categories represent potential separate property, the real key is whose name **title** to the property is in. If one spouse's name appears alone on the title to a car, that car is a separate asset of that spouse.

Joint **marital property** is that property acquired by the couple while they were married. Almost, but not all, property bought while married is joint marital property. Joint marital property is *divided* based on the laws of each state. The state divides the property pursuant to either community property laws or equitable distribution laws.

COMMUNITY PROPERTY. As indicated, community property is a method of classifying property acquired (and debts incurred—see Chapter 12, "Marital Debts") during marriage. In a community property state, the marriage is often referred to as the community, and an asset bought by the community is called a community asset. All property classified as community assets are divided equally at divorce.

In community property states, generally speaking, all assets acquired by either spouse during marriage belong to *both* spouses equally. In fact, in most community property states, the law presumes that any asset acquired during marriage is a community asset.

> Mark had a great job as a television director. He made good money and enjoyed his work. After they were married, Mark and Jennifer bought a house using both their credit. Mark contributed 90 percent of the down payment, and Jennifer put in 10 percent. When they divorced three years later, the court awarded Jennifer 50 percent of the house, as it was a community asset.

Almost everything acquired by the community during the marriage becomes a community asset. Even if you make $100,000 a year and your husband stays home with the kids, everything you buy while married is usually half his.

You can tell whether an asset is separate or community by looking at the time of acquisition. If acquired during marriage, it is presumed community; if not, then not. One exception to this rule is if the item was purchased while married, but one spouse used money that can be *traced to a separate source* to buy it. Then it likely will be considered separate property. For example, if a wife who had a separate trust fund set up before her marriage uses that money to buy a car while married, a court would likely consider that car her separate property.

If the spouse who has separate funds is not very careful, however, any property bought with that money could very easily end up as community, and not separate, property. This is due to the concept known as **commingled property**. Commingling occurs when separate funds and community funds, or even two separate funds of each mate, are mingled together (in the same bank account, for instance). Any property bought with commingled funds is usually considered a community asset. The property loses all separate characteristics when bought with commingled money.

Aside from mixing money in the same bank account, commingling could occur any time separate funds are mixed with community funds. For example, assume that the wife used that same trust fund to buy a car for herself. Three years later, she traded the car in and added another $3,000 of community money to buy a new car. Because her separate funds were mixed with community funds, the car is a commingled asset, and would likely be considered community property.

To the extent that a spouse can actually trace the funds back to a separate source, that spouse would be entitled to a reimbursement of that amount upon divorce. The general rule, though, remains: all property bought while married is presumed by law to be community property and is owned equally by both spouses.

Community property applies to earnings as well. All earnings made while married, and all property bought from those earnings, are considered community property.

Bill made $75,000 a year while Lisa stayed home with the children. Bill religiously saved 10 percent of his income every month. By the time they were divorced, he had $35,000 in the bank. Lisa owned half of it.

A professional degree, like a law or medical degree, is generally not considered a community asset, although a wife who put her husband through law school may disagree. The unfairness of that rule is self-evident: the wife suffers the relative poverty of law school, gets divorced, and then the husband receives the benefits of her contribution for a lifetime. That such a rule often creates unfair results is evidenced by the fact that many courts in community property states now award the spouse some type of reimbursement for her contribution to the degree. When the couple has enjoyed the fruits of the degree for some time (e.g., ten years), a court then assumes that both spouses have received benefits from the degree, and reimbursement is usually not given.

EQUITABLE DISTRIBUTION. In a community property state, almost everything acquired during marriage is split fifty-fifty, even if one spouse contributed more than the other. In the forty-one equitable distribution states and the District of Columbia, the court does not take such a mathematical approach. Instead, it attempts to divide the marital property fairly and equitably.

In an equitable distribution state, property acquired during marriage is often characterized by how title to the property is held. If title to the house is in the name of the husband, it will often be considered his during the marriage. Upon divorce, however, matters are different. Understand that the difference is in the distribution at divorce, not the acquisition during marriage. Community property states divide marital assets *equally* at divorce. Equitable distribution states divide marital assets *fairly*. Equal and fair are not the same thing.

When dividing the assets of a marriage, the court in an equitable distribution state will consider a variety of factors that are intended to create a fair, though not necessarily equal, result. Those factors include who holds title to the property, length of marriage, age, health, income, occupation, future earning capacity, present economic circumstances, pensions, debts and liabilities, possible alimony awards, and any misdeeds of a spouse leading to the divorce, (i.e., fault). The problem with this laundry list is that each judge takes and weighs different factors differently in an effort to be fair. The upshot is that the spouse who makes more usually gets more.

Pauline and Ralph lived in an equitable distribution state and were getting divorced after twelve years of marriage. Ralph precipitated the divorce by drinking too much, staying out too late, and ignoring the children. Pauline's position as a horse trainer was more lucrative than Ralph's sales job at an antique shop. While they were married, they bought a home, furniture, cars, and many antiques.

Because she made more, and could afford it, the court awarded the house to Pauline. Because of his love of, and expertise in, antiques, Ralph was given the majority of those. Although the cars were divided equally, Ralph received little furniture due to his "fault."

Just like community property states, equitable distribution states keep separate property separate. The risk of commingling is equally great as well. The separate property of one spouse can easily become the marital property of both spouses unless precise records are kept.

TAKING THE RISK OUT OF THE DIVISION PROCESS. Under either of the two systems discussed above, the risk remains the same: it is a judge who decides what is "equal" and what is "fair." Having a third party divide your property is akin to letting someone tell you how to raise your kids—while he may have some good ideas, his values are not your values. A judge's idea of fair and equal may be vastly different from your own. You never know what a judge or jury will do.

But the judge need not be the one to make the decision. You can make it without him. In fact, 90 percent of all divorces are settled out of court, with the parties themselves figuring out how to divide their assets, pay alimony, and raise their children. Once you know what kind of property division state you live in, you can figure out whose property is whose, and then set about the task of dividing that property. A **property settlement** is part of an overall **marriage settlement agreement** agreed and entered into between the parties. The marriage settlement agreement can cover much more than just property—namely, finances, alimony, visitation, child support, and child custody. It should be your goal to try to settle all outstanding issues in your case and leave nothing to chance. This obviates the need for trial.

The court will review any property settlement entered into between spouses to make sure it meets certain standards, but it almost always accepts the agreement as negotiated. Although working with the person you are divorcing may seem daunting, remember: if you cannot decide how to divide your property, the judge can.

The Important Legal Concept to Remember: Property is defined either at the time of purchase or by whose name is on the title, depending upon the state. Property acquired during marriage is often jointly owned marital property. While some states divide this property equally, and others fairly, you can divide it pretty much any way you want to.

9

PROPERTY DIVISION, PART I: PREPARATION

How to divide property

Hidden assets

Getting started

HOW TO DIVIDE PROPERTY. In order to divide property in a way that works (that is, one that gets you most of what you want), you first need to know what you own and owe, and what you're worth. It is at the same time not as simple as it sounds and usually more work than anticipated. It is vital nonetheless. Without a clear picture of your financial state, it is impossible to negotiate a settlement. Hence the need for preparation.

The first thing to do is to make a list of assets, divided into three sections, labeled mine, his (or hers), and ours. The preceding chapter should help you figure out whose property is whose. Inventory everything you own and put each item in one section, along with an estimated value.

Besides large items such as cars and homes, the list should include all personal property, such as appliances, furniture, books, etc. Financial assets too should be accounted for. This would include stocks, bonds, CDs, annuities, mutual funds, treasury bills, bank accounts, IRAs, life insurance (whole life insurance can be cashed out, term life insurance has no cash value), jewelry, real estate, limited partnerships, and any other investments. Each asset must be given a value. (If a certain item is difficult to gauge, see the next chapter for valuation methods.) For example:

ASSETS

MINE	VALUE
Skis	$200
Guns	300
Stereo	100

HERS	
Skis	$ 200
1986 Subaru	4,000

OURS	
House	$10,000 (worth $100,000, owe $90,000)
1995 Honda	5,000 (worth $12,000, owe $7,000)
Furniture	1,000
IRA	3,000

Next, make a list of all debts and liabilities, including mortgages, credit cards, student loans, car loans, taxes, bills, and personal loans.

DEBTS

MINE	AMOUNT OWED
Student loan	$10,000

HERS	
Student loan	$10,000
Credit cards	5,000

OURS

House	$90,000
1995 Honda	7,000
Credit cards	5,000
Taxes	500

After listing both assets and debts, a final list needs to be made of your current monthly budget and a projection of expenses after divorce. This will be immensely helpful when it comes time to negotiate. If you know that your income will drop by two-thirds when your spouse moves out, you may be less likely to fight for the house and expensive mortgage. You may instead be more inclined to let her stay in the house and buy you out.

HIDDEN ASSETS. One thing that sometimes happens early in the property division process is that one spouse attempts to hide what he owns, or his mate thinks that he is doing so. And there is often a good reason for this: people getting divorced can act crazy, doing things they normally would not do.

Thinking that if they are able to keep the asset from their mate they won't have to share it, divorcing mates sometimes try many stupid things borne of greed and anger—cashing out accounts, opening new accounts under false names, sending money to overseas banks, burying money in the backyard, transferring property to dummy partnerships or friends, etc.

It is a risky thing to do because the results can be disastrous. The risks are basically threefold. First, there is the risk of criminal sanctions. Before a divorce is ever finalized, each spouse will sign or swear under penalty of perjury that he or she has told the truth and has hidden nothing. If assets have been hidden, then perjury is being committed when that oath is taken. Perjury is a felony. If the hidden assets are ever discovered, sanctions include heavy fines, jail time, or both.

The second problem when someone tries to hide assets is that his spouse almost always finds out. When that happens, she will make her husband's life more difficult than it already is. Any hope of working things out and keeping expenses down will be gone. Aside from these soaring legal costs, bills might not be paid, property might become vandalized, and other assets may be depleted. Thus, a real risk of bankruptcy exists for those who are caught hiding assets. Many bankruptcies are filed by divorced people who could not afford the $20,000 legal bill that came due after their hardball tactics failed.

The final risk is that if caught, not only will one's mate make life difficult, but the judge will too. Once a judge finds out that one of the parties tried to hide an asset, punishment will be swift and severe. The cheater may lose the property altogether, and, more important, he could lose custody or visitation rights to his children.

If you suspect that your spouse is hiding something, it is not that difficult to locate the assets, although it can be expensive. The first thing to do is to hire a private investigator. A private investigator can run a very effective computer and asset check, which will allow him to trace hidden money and property. A good hint is to check loan applications from previous loans obtained by your spouse since these applications list assets, bank accounts, income, etc. Personal and business tax returns should be reviewed, as should stock statements. Check also to see if any bank accounts were opened in your children's names.

Your lawyer should use the discovery procedures available to request documents such as bank statements, credit card state-ments, title transfers, and the like. As your spouse will have to sign the response under penalty of perjury (again), document production requests often prove to be a useful tool. You should also take the **deposition** of anyone you suspect may have knowledge of any tricky transfers. Secretaries, friends, and business associates are far more reluctant to perjure themselves than greedy spouses are.

GETTING STARTED. After all lists have been made and all assets are accounted for, it is time to get down to the nitty-gritty, often

ugly, sometimes demeaning, rarely satisfying process of negotiating with your soon-to-be ex. The property settlement and
overall marriage settlement agreement can be worked out either
on your own, with the assistance of attorneys, or through some
type of mediation process. (See Chapter 20, "Mediation.")

You may find as negotiations proceed that some issues are
resolved fairly easily and others not at all. That is fine. It is
possible to settle some issues in your case (e.g., property) and
go to trial on the remaining ones (e.g., child custody). While
not necessarily desirable, it is neither altogether terrible.

**The Important Legal Concept to Remember: Preparation
and investigation are the keys to dividing property in a way
that ensures protection and fairness.**

10

PROPERTY DIVISION, PART II: DIVIDING THE PROPERTY

Separate property
Personal property
The house
The family business
Financial investments
Retirement benefits

SEPARATE PROPERTY. The first thing to do, and the easy part, is to take the things on your list that are clearly yours, and give your spouse those things that are clearly his. Likewise, both parties need to accept responsibility for their respective debts. (Division of marital debts is discussed in Chapter 12, "Marital Debts 12.")

PERSONAL PROPERTY. The next easiest thing to divide is personal property—things like furniture, jewelry, cars, televisions and stereos, hobby equipment, etc. Whereas larger items like homes and retirement accounts must be valued fairly precisely, often by an expert, that need not occur here. Both spouses know what their personal property is worth compared to other property. Dividing these assets is really not much more than an exercise in bartering and negotiation. (For more information on negotiating with your spouse, see Chapter 21, "How to Negotiate a Great Deal.")

THE HOUSE. There are three different ways to divide a family residence; however, before utilizing any of them, you must have a realistic value placed on the house. You can figure out the **fair market value** of your home either by hiring an independent appraiser or by checking out what realtors call comparable home sales, i.e., the selling price of a house similar to yours in your neighborhood that has recently been sold. Talk to a realtor to get a list of comparable home sales or check out some houses for yourself. Either way, you need to know what your house is worth before you can figure out what to do with it.

The three methods are as follows:

1. *One of the parties keeps the house:* Under this plan, one partner keeps the house and buys out the other spouse. The one who sells his share to the mate who is keeping the property will receive a share of the **equity** in the home. Determining equity is easy: subtract how much you owe from what the house is worth. If $150,000 is owed and the house can sell for $200,000, then there is $50,000 in equity. The spouse being bought out gets half—$25,000.

   The financial inability to buy out the other spouse should not pose a problem. Methods of financing the buyout include refinancing or selling a portion of the house to a third person. Another option is to barter with your mate. For example:

   > Sarah decided she wanted to stay in the house. She therefore needed to pay Sam $50,000 for his share of the equity, which she did not have. What she did have was $500 a month in alimony coming from Sam for the next five years. She agreed to forgo the money ($500 x 60 months = $30,000), and gave him $20,000 in other property. As a

result, Sarah owned the home outright without paying Sam any out-of-pocket money.

A real advantage for the person being bought out is that the money received is not taxed by the IRS since it constitutes a property sale "incident to divorce." As opposed to the next option, the tax savings can be significant. (See Chapter 15, "Divorce and Taxes.")

2. *Neither party keeps the house:* If the couple cannot agree on who will get the home, or if neither party wants the memories associated with it, then a second option is to sell the house and split the proceeds. Selling the house will eat into the equity, though. Figure that selling costs will be roughly 8 percent of the selling price.

Henry and Gina decided to sell the house and split the profits. Since they had owned the house for two years, they had only $10,000 in equity. When the house sold for $100,000, they were expecting $5,000 each. They did not anticipate that fees and costs would gobble up 8 percent—$8,000. They each got $1,000 in the end.

If the house has appreciated in value, anticipate that there will be a significant **capital gains tax** if the money is not reinvested again within two years (at least under the present tax code). The IRS, not surprisingly, considers the sale of a home a taxable event. Unlike a spousal buyout, as outlined above, divorce is irrelevant when computing this tax.

In a community property state, if left up to a judge, the proceeds from the sale of a home would be split evenly. In an equitable distribution state, the split may not be fifty-fifty. Since property division is supposed to be "fair" in those states, the higher wage earner often gets more of the proceeds since the judge usually assumes that he put more money into the home.

3. *Both spouses keep the house:* A final option is to continue to own the home together and rent it out. This may be attractive when real estate prices are low. The problem, of course, is that if you cannot live with this person, you may find it difficult being business partners with him as well.

Finally, when deciding what to do with the house, there is an important tax law to know about if you are fifty-five or older. As has been discussed, there is the possibility of a large tax bite on the profits on the sale of the house. The IRS code allows individuals fifty-five or older a one-time exclusion on house sales that net up to $125,000 in profit. That means that you can sell the house, make a profit of $125,000, and pay no capital gains tax on it.

THE FAMILY BUSINESS. Besides the home, a family business may be the most valuable marital asset. If both partners were involved in running the business, it may be very difficult to divide, as both will probably want it. And even if only one spouse ran the business, the other still likely has some interest in it.

In community property states, if the business was started after the marriage, then it is a community asset, owned fifty-fifty. This is true even if only one spouse was involved in it. In an equitable distribution state, the one who ran the business will likely be given it by the courts, so any settlement should take that into account.

Under any of these scenarios—community property versus equitable distribution; one spouse versus both spouses running the business—the main issue will be the value of the business. Valuing a business is difficult and should not be done by amateurs.

The best way to value the business is to hire a specialist called a business appraiser. As with hiring an attorney, word of mouth is the best way to find a good appraiser. Absent that, try the chamber of commerce, the Better Business Bureau, or the Yellow Pages. Expect the appraisal to cost several thousand dollars.

Many factors are taken into account when determining the value of a business, including comparable sales, profitability, years in existence, **goodwill**, location, future outlook, and leases, just to name a few. After examining all relevant information, the appraiser will submit a report, which gives a value for the business and explains how that figure was calculated.

Once you have that, it is "just" a matter of dividing the business pie. Any of the methods mentioned previously to divide the house can be used to divide the business, but, in all likelihood, one person will buy out the other.

FINANCIAL INVESTMENTS. Financial investments are more than savings accounts and stocks. Other investments include college funds, bonds, CDs, annuities, mutual funds, treasury bills, IRAs, life insurance, and limited partnerships. Each of these must be valued and divided. No one said getting divorced would be easy.

Some of these assets are easy to value, others are not. Many have values listed in every statement, such as checking, savings, and many investment accounts. Check mutual fund and other investment account statements or talk to a broker.

Once all investments have been valued and accounted for, it is time to divvy up the portfolio. Aside from assessing the value of each asset, a financial counselor can also advise which assets are worth keeping and which are smart to trade away. Make sure to barter for investments that you know you can live with as a single person. Will you be able to afford the mortgage? Do you know when to sell stock?

RETIREMENT BENEFITS. If you have a retirement plan from work, your spouse likely has an interest in it, and vice versa. Determining the value of the plan—be it a 401(k), a Keogh, or a profit-sharing plan—is difficult. By its very nature, a retirement plan is not supposed to pay dividends until retirement.

Figuring out the present dollar value of a future payout is a problem compounded by the fact that plans differ and state laws differ as to how much interest spouses have in each other's retirement benefits. Nevertheless, there are several ways to figure out what a plan is worth:

- *Hire a professional:* An **actuary** is a statistician or economist who computes the present value of retirement plans. Investment counselors, financial planners, and bankers can also help. This is the best method.

- *Talk to the plan administrator:* Every retirement plan has a person who administers it. While he does not have the expertise of an actuary, whose actual job includes analyzing retirement benefit plans, he is probably well informed enough to make a good estimate of the plan's present worth.

- *Do it yourself:* This is by far the least advisable method. Employment retirement plans are complicated, period. If you must do it yourself, then the simplest way is to get a schedule of contributions from the plan administrator and figure out how much was contributed during the marriage. While this will give you the present value of the plan, it does not give the value of the plan at retirement. A plan that may pay out $100,000 in retirement benefits in twenty years may be worth only $20,000 in present-day dollars. Nevertheless, once contributions are accounted for, you can calculate how much of the plan was paid while married. Each spouse is then likely entitled to 50 percent of the present dollar value paid into the plan while married. Again, the major problem with this method is that *it does not take into account the future value of the plan.* Be smart—hire an actuary.

Once the plan is valued, then either one spouse buys the other out or something else is bartered for it in exchange. If the spouse being bought out requests it, she can get a **Qualified Domestic Relations Order** (a QDRO). The QDRO tells the plan administrator how the plan is to be allocated between the divorcing couple. The nonemployee spouse will usually be awarded a lump sum equal to his calculated present-day share of the plan.

Social Security and military pensions generally are not considered joint retirement plans, and thus are not usually part of a property settlement. An exception to both occurs when one spouse is nonworking and the couple was married for at least ten years. In that case, federal law, which controls both Social Security and military pensions, allows for benefits to be granted to the nonworking partner. Some military benefits, however, do not accrue until twenty years of marriage. It just depends.

The Important Legal Concept to Remember: The key to dividing large assets is to obtain assessments that correctly reflect the true value of the property. Once this is done, it is a matter of trading and exchanging the property.

11

PROPERTY DIVISION, PART III: A TYPICAL PROPERTY DIVISION

What follows is an example of a property settlement. To make this example easier to understand, it is assumed that each partner paid for half of each item. In a community property state this is assumed. In an equitable distribution state it is not.

Susie and Spencer still owe $100,000 toward their home, which is worth $200,000. Spencer has a pension plan from work worth $39,000, which he has paid into for fifteen years (ten while married to Susie). Susie owns a business worth $25,000, which she started after she married Spencer. They jointly own a mutual fund worth $30,000. They have furniture and other joint personal property worth $5,000, and each has separate property—Susie's is worth $5,000; Spencer's, $1,000.

The first thing to notice is that each item has a value. It would be impossible to divide the property fairly without knowing what it is worth.

Starting with the easy things, Susie and Spencer would each get their own separate property, and even though the value is unequal, there is nothing "joint" about the property, so neither has an interest in the other's.

The total value of all jointly owned items is $186,000. The equity in the house is $100,000 (its value, $200,000, less the amount owed, $100,000). The pension, although valued at $39,000, is only a partially joint asset since Spencer paid into it for five years while he was single. Thus, the marital share is ten of the fifteen years, or two thirds of its total value. Since its total present value is $39,000, the marital share is two thirds of that—$26,000. The other $13,000 in the plan is Spencer's separate property because he earned it while he was single. The business is worth $25,000 and is completely a marital asset since it was started during the marriage. The furniture is worth $5,000, and the mutual fund is worth $30,000—all joint.

ASSETS

SUSIE

$5,000 in personal property

SPENCER

$1,000 in personal property
$13,000 in pension

JOINT

House	$100,000
Pension plan	26,000
Business	25,000
Furniture, etc.	5,000
Mutual fund	30,000
Total	$186,000

The challenging part is dividing that $186,000 pie. If Susie wanted the house, then even if Spencer is given everything else, he still would get only $86,000. If Susie wanted to keep the house and her business—not an unreasonable request— Spencer would get almost nothing.

The dilemma is easily solved. First, each partner should take that item he or she wants most. Susie would get her business and Spencer would get his retirement. They are roughly equal in value: the business is worth $25,000; the retirement plan, $26,000. Susie would initially be short $500 since that would be the amount Spencer would need to give her to even things out. This could be remedied when they divide the mutual fund: instead of $15,000 each, Spencer could give Susie an extra $500. He would get $14,500; she would get $15,500. The $5,000 in joint personal property could be divided equally.

What will they do with the house? Therein lies the rub. If Spencer really wants it, then he would have to pay Susie $50,000. He could try to refinance it in order to pay Susie, though that may prove to be difficult. Spencer might have a hard time qualifying for a loan since, without Susie's paycheck, his income will be cut in half upon his divorce. He could take out a second mortgage on the house, but again he would face the problem of qualifying. He could sell part of the house to a third party and use the proceeds to pay Susie, or he could give her all of his retirement and then some in order to finance the buyout. Another problem that may arise for Spencer would be the inability to pay the mortgage even if he does get the house.

The property settlement stated that Spencer would get the house and take out a second mortgage to pay Susie for her half of the equity. A week after the divorce was final, Spencer was fired from his job and could not qualify for a loan. He eventually declared bankruptcy, and Susie never got her money.

Instead of Spencer trying to pay the large mortgage alone, an easier option for them would be to sell the property and split the proceeds. Both Spencer and Susie would end up with money in the bank at a time when that would be very useful.

The Important Legal Concept to Remember: Dividing property is a matter of correctly valuing property, working together, and being creative.

IV

MONEY

12

MARITAL DEBTS

Types of debts
Dividing debts
Debts and bankruptcy

TYPES OF DEBTS. Like property, debts too are split up at divorce. There are three types of debts that you need to be aware of when divorcing since each is handled a little differently. Those three types are debts incurred by each spouse before marriage, debts incurred by the couple while married, and debts incurred by each spouse after separation. The type of debt determines how it will be divided as part of a marriage settlement agreement or trial.

In both community property and equitable distribution states, debts incurred before marriage remain the responsibility of the person who incurred the debt. These are separate debts. This means that should the debtor spouse default on a premarital obligation, the nondebtor spouse's money and property cannot be used to pay the debt.

Debts incurred by either spouse while married are joint debts—both spouses are responsible for them and any settlement must split them evenly. Say, however, that the husband bought a boat while he was married but used money from a separate bank account for the down payment. In all likelihood, a court would consider that a separate debt (and separate property) and would award both to the husband. Otherwise, the general rule is that all debts incurred while married are joint, and must be assigned to one spouse or the other at divorce.

The last type of potential debt are those in that musty gray area that are incurred after the separation but before the divorce is final. No broad statement can be made as to the law in this area—state laws differ greatly. While some states conclude that each party is responsible for his or her own post-separation debts, others mandate that both parties remain jointly responsible until a settlement is signed. Still others conclude that only debts incurred for necessities (food and clothing) are joint during this period.

DIVIDING DEBTS. In community property states, joint debts are divided equally; each mate is responsible for half of the marital debts. In equitable distribution states, the debts are divided equitably and fairly, so that the partner more able to pay is assigned more of the debts (and more property too). Joint debts include things like credit cards, car loans, mortgages, taxes, and monthly bills.

Regardless of whether you are in a community property or an equitable distribution state, if you and your mate agree, you can divide your debts (and your property) any way you like. You must take extreme caution when dividing your debts. Even more than dividing property, the debt division process is a critical negotiation in a divorce and can have the most severe long-term effects.

David and Kim parted amicably, were able to settle their differences quickly, and divided their property and debts easily. David took responsibility for $10,000 of the joint credit card debt. After everything was signed, David found out that Kim had slept with his best friend. David stopped making payments on the credit card debt and the creditors came after Kim. Although Kim sent copies of the settlement agreement to them to prove that the debt was David's responsibility, they did not care. Marriage settlement agreements are not binding on anyone other than the parties who sign them. The credit card companies sued David and Kim, and Kim ended up having her wages garnished to pay the debt.

It bears repeating: *marriage settlement agreements are not binding on anyone other than the two parties who sign them.*

There are basically three options when dividing marital debts: they can be divided equally, they can be given primarily to one spouse in exchange for getting more property, or they can be paid off before the divorce is finalized.

The risk experienced above by Kim can occur when either of the first two options are utilized. If your husband takes responsibility for any of the debts, you really have no way to police him. If he chooses not to, or cannot, pay the money owed, it is you whom the creditors will come after. That is why the third option of a payoff is both the best and the least risky choice. If the debts can be paid off, either by selling assets or by consolidating them into one payment that you would be responsible for (again, in exchange for extra property), then you can be assured that the debts will be paid. For example:

Rick and Beth had $30,000 in assets and $10,000 in debts. Instead of dividing everything in half—assets and debts alike—they decided to cash out their savings account and pay the debts. Each walked away with $10,000 of property.

Or:

Rick and Beth had $30,000 in assets and $10,000 in debts. Beth was worried that Rick would not pay his half of the debts, so she agreed to take responsibility for the entire amount. The marriage settlement agreement assigned all debts to her, $5,000 of which were Rick's. Instead of dividing the property in half, she also received $5,000 in extra property to even out the additional $5,000 in debt she took on. Rick received no debt, and $10,000 in property, and Beth got $10,000 in debts and $20,000 in property.

DEBTS AND BANKRUPTCY. After a divorce, many people end up saddled with debts, payments, and bills they cannot pay. It is not that they planned it that way; it just seems to be the nature of the divorce beast. Attorney fees, combined with the reduction from double to single wage-earner income, are the most prevalent reasons. Another reason, as indicated, is the former spouse who fails to pay her share of the agreed-upon debts, thereby forcing the creditors to come after the other spouse. Bankruptcy is a common byproduct of divorce.

There are two types of bankruptcies available for people contemplating such a move: Chapter 7 and Chapter 13. Chapter 7 is what most people think of when they think about bankruptcy. Under a Chapter 7, most debts are not paid back and are wiped out when the bankruptcy is over (usually about four months). Under a Chapter 13 bankruptcy, the debtor pays her obligations back monthly through a bankruptcy trustee. Chapter 13 is usually used by small businesses that want to reorganize and by individuals who have debts that do not fit the Chapter 7 requirements (things like mortgage **arrearages**). For most divorcing debtors, a Chapter 7 is usually the best way to go.

Not all debts can be extinguished (the legal term is **discharged**) in a Chapter 7. There are basically two kinds of debts you can have: secured and unsecured. A secured debt is a debt secured by a piece of property. The easiest way to think of it is as **collateral**. The bank gives home loans only if the house is used as collateral. That's a secured debt. A car loan is another type of secured debt. The bank loans you the money, but the car is considered collateral until the loan is paid back. Secured debts are not easily eliminated in a bankruptcy. The only choice you essentially have is either to keep making the payments or to give the property back.

Conversely, unsecured debts are things like credit cards, doctor bills, utility bills, etc. There is no collateral associated with the granting of credit. Unsecured debts are easily discharged in bankruptcy. You could owe $50,000 to eight different credit card companies and a Chapter 7 bankruptcy would wipe out the debt entirely.

You may also have debts incidental to the divorce—things like alimony, property installment payments, and child support payments. These kinds of support obligations are generally not dischargable in a bankruptcy. Because so many divorced husbands were creatively eliminating their divorce obligations in bankruptcy, the Bankruptcy Code was amended in 1994 to forbid such actions. It is now all but impossible to rid oneself of divorce obligations in a Chapter 7.

Bankruptcy is certainly an effective way to start over when you have gotten in over your head financially. Needless to say, the downside is a negative credit rating for ten years. But when compared to harassing phone calls, nasty letters, wage garnishments, and $20,000 in credit card debt, a negative credit rating may not look so bad. (For more information, see the companion book, *Ask a Lawyer: Debt and Bankruptcy*.)

The Important Legal Concept to Remember: The problem with dividing debts is that there is no enforcement mechanism that ensures that both parties will live up to their obligations. The best advice is, if at all possible, pay the debts before the divorce is over.

13

ALIMONY AND SPOUSAL SUPPORT

How the court determines alimony
Types of alimony
Methods of payment
If your mate stops making payments
Modification
Termination

In the past twenty years the idea behind alimony has changed. Whereas it used to be considered an almost automatic "right" for the wife to receive alimony from her husband upon divorce, that is not the case today. Alimony is now far more limited, and not even granted in many divorces. The reason is that women are now an integral part of the workforce, and therefore the idea behind alimony payments—support for the non-breadwinner—no longer holds true.

This is not to say that alimony has disappeared—far from it. It is just that spousal support payments are now usually for less time and money than before. The idea behind alimony today is to give the spouse who earns less—still usually the wife—a chance to get on her feet financially and become self-supporting.

HOW THE COURT DETERMINES ALIMONY. Because the financial situation of each couple getting divorced is unique, courts tend not to use rigid guidelines or formulas when awarding spousal support. Instead they look to several factors, weighing each, and then make a corresponding award. Those factors are

- *Need:* If one of the partners will obviously need some time and help before she can become financially self-sufficient, then spousal support is more likely. Has that spouse been working? Does she have marketable skills? Are there children at home who need a mother there? How much does this spouse need to live on? Answers to these types of questions establish need. If both spouses have been working and make roughly the same amount of money, there is less need and spousal support is less likely.

- *Ability to pay:* If one spouse makes more than the other and therefore has the ability to make payments, an alimony award is more likely. An attempt by the spouse who will likely pay to reduce net income by taking a lesser paying job rarely works. Courts not only usually see through the sham but can punish the charlatan financially as well.

- *The manner of living to which the couple has become accustomed:* The rich get more spousal support for two reasons. First, they can afford to pay more (see above). Second, they are used to spending more. Lifestyle is as big a factor in awarding alimony in some cases as anything else.

- *Length of marriage:* Short marriages, say, two years or less, rarely result in alimony. Long marriages of ten years or more almost always do.

- *Age and health of the parties:* Young people pay less, older people pay more. Healthy people pay more, sick people get more.

TYPES OF ALIMONY. The two types of alimony are temporary and permanent. Temporary alimony is awarded by the court after divorce papers have been filed pending the final decree, or **judgment**. It is obtained by bringing a **motion** before the court requesting the temporary assistance. Temporary alimony is intended to help a spouse take care of necessities while the proceedings continue.

Permanent alimony is an oxymoron; it is rarely, if ever, permanent. As indicated previously, so-called permanent alimony is usually for a set amount of time. The only time that it may actually last indefinitely is when the spouses have been married for many years and the wife (almost always) is older and has no marketable skills. Even indefinite alimony will end if the recipient remarries or if the payer dies.

Another type of alimony, although not really alimony, is called palimony. *Palimony* is a word used to describe alimony and property division for *unmarried couples*. It is a term that came of age in the 1970s, when many couples started living together instead of marrying. It was coined in 1976 when Michelle Triola Marvin sued her ex-boyfriend, actor Lee Marvin, for support and division of property earned during the six years the couple lived together. Her suit alleged that they had entered into an oral agreement in which the actor had agreed to divide the property earned while they were together, and that he had further agreed to take care of Ms. Marvin for life. Lee Marvin contended that since they were not married, he owed her nothing.

The California Supreme Court held that unmarried couples could legally enter into such palimony agreements, be they oral or written, and, if proven at trial, such agreements are binding. This ruling applied to both heterosexual and homosexual couples and has been adopted by most states in one form or another. (After the case was sent back to trial court, the judge awarded Ms. Marvin $104,000. This sum was later overturned, again by the California Supreme Court. Ms. Marvin got nothing.)

A person wishing to establish a palimony award will need to go to court and prove that the other mate promised support in exchange for services (although the services *cannot* be sexual since that would constitute prostitution). For example, say that Marty and Sandy agreed to live together, and decided that

Sandy would work outside the home and take care of all expenses while Marty stayed home with the kids. This agreement is likely a valid contract that would entitle Marty to pal-imonious monetary and property rights if the couple split up.

METHODS OF PAYMENT. Although most people think of begrudgingly made monthly payments when they think of alimony, there are several ways to structure an alimony award. Of course the most common is the monthly payment made for a set period of time. Once all the payments are made, the obligation ceases. For the receiving spouse, it is a comfort; for the paying spouse, a pain. Even though monthly checks should provide the receiving spouse with security, such is not always the case.

> The marital settlement agreement mandated that Bill would pay Karen $250 per month for three years as spousal support, and $250 per month in child support until all the children turned eighteen. One month after the divorce was final, Bill stopped all spousal support payments, although he continued to make his child support payments regularly and on time. Karen took him back to court two times before finally giving up.

Counting on an ex to do anything he says he will do is fraught with danger. Not only might he stop paying debts that were assigned to him (see Chapter 12, "Marital Debts"), but he might also stop making scheduled alimony or child support payments. The sad fact is that an ex-spouse has little incentive to make any payments, besides the long arm of the law.

Because of this, it might be advisable to structure an alimony award as one lump sum rather than as monthly payments, if at all possible. It really benefits both parties. For the receiving spouse, the risk of noncompliance is taken out of the equation once a lump sum is paid. Lump sum payments are often in the best interests of the spouse who will be paying the money as well. Few things in life are less satisfying than making out checks every month to an ex-wife. The lump sum eliminates that. Moreover, the lump sum amount can be negotiated to be less than the total combined monthly payments would have been since that is a fair exchange for coming up with a large amount all at once. Not every state allows lump sum support payments, and you will need to consult with a lawyer to determine if this is possible in your case.

A final way to take care of alimony, besides monthly or lump sum payments, is for the spouse who is due the money to take property instead. Future alimony worth $15,000 might be bartered for a $10,000 car today.

IF YOUR MATE STOPS MAKING PAYMENTS. If your alimony award is scheduled to be made in monthly payments, as most are, and your mate has stopped making the scheduled payments, the results can be severe. Courts do not take kindly to being ignored, and violating the final divorce decree or judgment is blatant disregard for the rule of law.

If this has happened, you need to bring it to the court's attention. The court has several tools available for bringing a deadbeat mate to task and will use them. Your ex-spouse's wages can be attached and applied to the amount due (a **wage garnishment**); his bank accounts can be attached (a **levy**); his home can be attached (a **lien**); his property can be seized (a **seizure**). Furthermore, since alimony is part of a court order, refusal to pay constitutes **contempt of court**, and contempt of court is a crime. Your spouse can end up in jail.

Finally, if the spouse who owes the money lives in another state, a law called the Revised Uniform Reciprocal Enforcement of Support Act (RURESA) allows one state to enforce a judgment from a different state, even though the states may have different spousal support laws. Whatever method is utilized, know that enforcing the judgment will be expensive and time-consuming, but should ultimately be successful.

MODIFICATION. It is possible to have the award modified higher or lower down the road. Modification can be either temporary or permanent. Again, however, it depends upon the state. Some states forbid alimony modifications altogether.

If the paying spouse suffers a temporary setback such as a medical problem, a financial crisis, or the like, a request can be made to the court to decrease the payments temporarily until the problem is resolved. Once that spouse is able to resume normal payments, the temporary modification will cease.

In those states that do allow permanent modification, it is necessary to present the court with a *reason* why modification is necessary, above and beyond a mere dislike for the original award. A **change in circumstances** is what is necessary— decreased ability to pay, a loss of a job, retirement, decreased need, an inheritance, the recipient moving in with a lover, birth of a new child, and so forth. Any major life change that affects the financial ability of the paying spouse or the need of the recipient spouse would likely constitute a change of circumstances resulting in a change of the amount paid. A major exception to this rule is when the spouse who pays remarries; in that case, the ex-wife cannot usually use the new wife's income to argue that the ex-husband can, and therefore should, pay more.

TERMINATION. Termination is automatic once the time for payments has expired, upon the death of the payer, or upon the remarriage of the recipient. If the recipient moves in with a lover and cohabits as if married, this too is grounds for possible termination.

The Important Legal Concept to Remember: Alimony forces two people who want nothing to do with each other to continue their relationship for as long as the alimony is supposed to be paid. It is usually better for everyone concerned to resolve alimony issues as quickly as possible.

14

CHILD SUPPORT

THE PURPOSE OF CHILD SUPPORT. Although not every ex-spouse needs monetary assistance after a divorce, every child does. Thus, unlike spousal support, child support is mandatory. Since it is a requirement *owed to the child* rather than to the spouse, it is normally awarded in every divorce that involves children.

The need for child support is obvious. After a divorce, when children are living in a single-parent household, there is far less money available to pay for necessities like food, clothing, and health insurance. And when the parents can afford it, and the children may have come to expect it, child support can include things like summer camp, private school, special medical needs, and other so-called luxury items. Child support is the law's way of simultaneously ensuring that parental obligations are fulfilled and the needs of children are met.

As explained in more detail in Chapter 16, "Child Custody," there are two types of custody: physical and legal. As a general rule, the parent who has physical custody (that is, the parent with whom the children live) is also the parent who receives child support. Because child support is an obligation owed by both spouses, even if one mate makes less money than the other, if she does not have custody, she will still likely have to pay support to the other spouse.

HOW THE COURT DETERMINES CHILD SUPPORT. The amount of support you should expect to pay or receive depends upon a variety of factors. First of all, family law is a creature of individual state law and each state is different. To reduce these differences, Congress passed the Family Support Act in 1988. Along with the Child Support Enforcement Act of 1984, states are now required to use federal guidelines when calculating the amount of child support awards. Some states use the factors below broadly, others narrowly. Some have mathematical formulas based on the factors, others have none.

- *The ability to pay:* The first thing a court will look at is the noncustodial parent's **net income,** which is the amount of money actually taken home every month. Net income is based on more than just employment—Social Security income, investment income, indeed all income, goes into the equation. The court will look at the occupation and earning capacity of each parent. The more you make, the more they take.

- *Needs of the child:* It is no secret that children are expensive. The court will look at things like educational, physical, medical, and emotional needs, day-care costs, and the age of the children. Special needs children will assuredly require more financial assistance than so-called normal children. Four children will need more money than one child.

- *Standard of living:* The court will also look at the standard of living of the spouses and the children.

- *Amount of time in each home:* The custody arrangement may play a large role in the size of the award. If a child lives primarily in one home, the noncustodial spouse will likely pay more. If custody is shared, the amount paid will be less.

IF YOUR MATE STOPS MAKING PAYMENTS. Failure to pay child support is probably the most serious financial violation possible in family law, and is dealt with accordingly. Civil penalties and criminal liability await those who take this path.

If you are not receiving child support payments from your ex, the first thing to do is to attempt to work it out without lawyers and courts. Armed with the possible ramifications outlined below, it may be possible to scare an ex-spouse into paying. Not many people want to risk jail time in order to save a couple of hundred bucks.

If that does not work, then the proper authorities can be enlisted to aid in the fight. Because nonpayment of child support has reached almost epidemic proportions, Congress has mandated certain procedures that have dramatically increased payments and enforcement, such as

- *Using the local district attorney:* District attorneys of each state are now authorized by law to assist in the collection of past-due child support payments, called arrears or arrearages. If the parent refuses to cooperate with the district attorney, she could go to jail.

- *Going to court:* Courts can garnish wages, seize property, or even freeze or garnish Social Security and tax-return payments now in order to enforce a support award. If your spouse has moved to another state, your state court used to have no legal authority to enforce the award in the other state, but now it does.

TRACKING DOWN A DEADBEAT DAD. The Child Support Enforcement Act of 1984 created a network of government computers designed to assist district attorneys in locating deadbeat fathers (it can also be used to find a child who has been taken out of state). Each district attorney's office should have a child support enforcement unit, which can now tie into the national parent locator service, accessing records in the FBI, Social Security Administration, Department of Defense, Veterans Administration, and other governmental agencies. If that does not work, or if the missing parent is suspected to be closer to home, the district attorney's office can also tap into local Motor Vehicle, prison, tax, and unemployment records in order to find the parent. If all else fails, a private investigator can be utilized.

MODIFICATION. Like a modification in alimony or custody, a change in child support is commenced by bringing a motion before a judge. The motion must be based on a reason, and the reason must be based on a change in circumstances. Accordingly, modification can be either temporary or permanent, depending upon the circumstances.

Dan and Sylvia shared custody of their daughter, Neila, and Dan was obligated to pay Sylvia $250 a month in child support. He made the payments on the first of every month for ten years. When Neila was fifteen, she decided that she wanted to live in one house, and moved in with her mom. Dan refused to pay any extra money, and Sylvia took him back to court, citing the move as a change in circumstances. The judge agreed, and doubled Dan's child support.

Not surprisingly, the change must be significant. A change in economic circumstances is a fine reason to request a modification of child support. Either the spouse who pays has an increased ability to pay, or the recipient has an increased economic need. Examples necessitating a temporary change include medical or financial emergencies or loss of a job. Examples necessitating permanent modification include forced retirement, a new lower-paying job, or a disability.

Again, there needs to be a marked change for the court to grant the modification; a job that increases or decreases income by 10 percent will not do. Moreover, if the court suspects that the noncustodial spouse took a lesser-paying job in order to decrease his child support payments, no modification will be granted.

Besides changes in the parents' situations, if the needs of the child change, modification is also appropriate. For example, if it turns out that the child is dyslexic and needs special schooling, a court will likely make the paying spouse help out financially.

The Important Legal Concept to Remember: Child support is a payment for the child, not the spouse, and is mandatory. Failure to pay is serious, and legal authorities are prepared to enforce payments. If the circumstances of the parent or child change, the support award can be modified.

15

DIVORCE AND TAXES

Filing while separated
The effect of child support and alimony on taxes
Dependency exemption
Property transfers

FILING WHILE SEPARATED. There are several possible ways to file taxes while getting divorced: jointly, married filing separately, and head of household. Each has certain requirements and benefits.

· *Filing jointly:* There are several advantages to filing jointly. Both parties can share the child dependency exemption that year (although it will need to be assigned to one spouse or the other upon divorce, see below). Moreover, earned income tax credits, dependent care tax credits, spousal dependency exemptions, and spousal IRA contributions can be claimed only on a joint return. The risk in filing a joint return is that both spouses share equally all financial liability for the taxes and any penalties due. If one spouse is trying to cheat the IRS, the other becomes an accomplice.

In order for spouses to file joint returns while divorcing, they must remain legally married until December 31 of the tax year. If the divorce became final on November 15, a joint tax return cannot be filed for that tax year.

· *Married filing separately:* The main advantage to this filing status is that any tax liability and responsibility is separate, not joint. Again, the spouses must still be married on December 31 of the tax year to file this way.

· *Head of household:* There may be significant tax savings to the parent who files a head-of-household return. In order to file this way the requirements are (1) filing separate returns; (2) the children must live with the spouse filing this way more than 50 percent of the time; and (3) the head-of-household spouse must pay for more than 50 percent of the costs of raising the children.

THE EFFECT OF CHILD SUPPORT AND ALIMONY ON TAXES. The IRS taxes all *income*. Income is very broadly defined.

Bob was ordered to pay Deanna $750 per month in spousal support for five years. Although Bob deducted the expenditure from his taxes that first year, Deanna did not report the revenue as she was unaware that spousal support was considered income. After being assessed a large penalty by the IRS, Deanna did not make that mistake again.

It should be no surprise that the IRS considers spousal support taxable income to the recipient and deductible payments to the paying spouse.

Child support is a different matter. Since it is intended to pay for the children's expenses, the IRS does not consider child support "income" to the parent. As opposed to alimony, it is neither taxable nor deductible, and need not be reported as income.

DEPENDENCY EXEMPTION. IRS regulations also assume that the parent with whom the child lives for more than six months is the custodial parent, even though the final divorce decree may state otherwise. Accordingly, the custodial parent is allowed to claim the child as a dependent (and therefore claim an exemption).

While the IRS does not really care where the child actually

lives, what really gets them cranky is when both divorced parents claim a child as exempt. The rule is that there is only one exemption per child, and only the physical custodial parent can claim it in any given year.

The problem is that the dependency exemption is usually divided as part of the property settlement. If the custodial parent received the exemption, there is no problem. If the noncustodial parent received the exemption, all the custodial parent needs to do is to waive her right to the exemption by filling out IRS Form 8332, and the problem is solved.

PROPERTY TRANSFERS. Property transfers between husband and wife occurring within one year from the divorce are, surprisingly, nontaxable events. If a couple owned a house together and they transfer it to the wife at divorce, the transfer, otherwise a taxable event, is not taxed. This is significant. Imagine that the house the wife gets was bought for $100,000 and is now worth $200,000. That $100,000 capital gain which the wife received is not taxed. Note, however, that if the wife later tries to sell the house, her tax liability will be for the amount received above and beyond the *original price*, i.e., $100,000. It is only the transfer between the spouses at divorce that is not taxed. All subsequent transfers are.

Finally, the IRS code allows those individuals fifty-five and older a one-time exclusion on house sales that net up to $125,000 in profit. That means that even after the divorce, you can sell the house, make a profit of $125,000, and pay no tax on it.

The Important Legal Concept to Remember: Taxes are complicated, boring, and important. Not caring about the tax consequences of a divorce is akin to not thinking about the sales tax when buying a car. You may end up paying far more than you anticipated if it is ignored.

CHILDREN

16

CHILD CUSTODY

Types of custody
How custody is determined
How to get a court to grant you physical custody

Of the myriad problems and issues that emerge during divorce, child custody is surely the most vexing. While the cause is usually no more complicated than that both parents love and want the children, the effect is complicated indeed. Parents fight over the children, often making them pawns in a game without winners. Compounding the difficulties is the fact that neither parent is usually in his or her right mind during a divorce—feelings are frayed, anger abounds—and the needs of the children, while usually important, may not be paramount. When dealing with custody issues, remember that *the needs of the children should be paramount to all else!*

TYPES OF CUSTODY. There are four permutations to the custody equation: **physical** and **legal custody**, and **sole** and **joint custody**. When a court awards "custody," what that really means is that the parents are given a combination of these four possible types of custody.

Physical custody is where the child physically lives. Does he live with Mom or Dad or both? A determination that physical custody will be with the mother means that the child's primary residence will be with her. Yet physical custody need not be with one parent alone; it can be solely with one parent or it can be shared by both.

It is the decision about whether the child will be with one or both parents that determines the second permutation—sole or joint custody. Sole physical custody means that the child will live solely, or primarily, with one parent. The parent with whom the child primarily resides is called the **custodial parent**. When one parent is the sole physical custodial parent, the other parent is called the **noncustodial parent**. That parent will have visitation rights on weekends, summertime, etc. (See Chapter 19, "Visitation.")

Joint physical custody means that the children will spend equal amounts of time living with both parents. As opposed to sole physical custody, where the child primarily lives with one parent, in a joint custody arrangement, the children split their living between two homes. Joint physical custody is only possible when the parents live in close proximity to each other. It would be impossible to have, and no court would allow, a joint custody arrangement in which the parents live, say, fifty miles away from each other. It would be too disruptive on the kids.

Ella and Karl split up when their daughter, Julie, was only five. They decided to share physical custody so that Julie could see a lot of both of her parents. They each had her for one week at a time until she was eight, and then switched to each having her for two weeks until she was thirteen. The problem was that Ella was very authoritarian and Karl was very easygoing. Julie was growing up in two very different houses, with two different sets of values, two bikes, and two lives. She was a confused young lady. Although she wanted to live with her dad, she could not bear to tell her mom. When she turned fourteen, she attempted suicide. It was only after that nearly tragic event that Ella and Karl realized their schizophrenic arrangement did not work and Julie needed to live with Karl full-time.

Until recently, the trend in family law was to award physical custody jointly, thereby assuring that the children would have continued contact with both parents—an important goal for family law judges. Unfortunately, as illustrated above, shared physical custody turned out to be better in theory than in practice. Many states now prefer that the children live primarily with one parent.

Legal custody has nothing to do with where the child lives; instead it is the right of the parent to make medical, religious, educational, and all other important decisions regarding the children. Will the children be raised Jewish? Will they go to public or private school? It is the legal custodial parent who makes these types of decisions.

Like physical custody, legal custody too can be sole or joint. For the most part, legal custody is almost always joint, unless one parent has proven himself to be incapable of making such decisions. The law prefers that both parents remain active in a child's life, and joint legal custody is a way to try to ensure that.

These four possibilities, physical and legal, sole and joint, custody, can be arranged in different ways. Parents could have joint physical and joint legal custody, sole physical and joint legal custody, or sole physical and sole legal custody. It depends upon the parents, the children, and the circumstances. Sole physical and joint legal custody means that the children will live primarily with one parent but both parents will share in all important decisions. (In some states, physical and legal custody are the same; the parent with whom the child lives is the parent who has the right to make the important decisions regarding the child. In most states however, custody is divided into physical and legal.)

As discussed in more detail in Chapter 18, "Custody Disputes and Modification," no parenting arrangement is set in stone. Children may move from one house to another, parents may become incapable of making good decisions. Whatever the case, one problem shared by almost all joint custody arrangements is that they do not have a foreseeable end in sight, unless one considers eighteen years of age foreseeable. The couple is forced to work with one another for the child's welfare long after the divorce is over. Not only that, but even after the child turns eighteen, divorced spouses will be grandparents to the same grandchildren. Sometimes, divorce too is until death do you part.

HOW CUSTODY IS DETERMINED. Like property—in fact, like the rest of any divorce—the custody determination can and should be decided between the couple and the court should be left out of it if at all possible. This can be done only if the parents actively attempt to resolve their differences and work out a suitable marriage settlement agreement. The court will look closely at the arrangement the parents agree upon and make sure that the child's best interests are met by the parenting arrangement.

Indeed, a term you should become intimately knowledgeable about is the **best interests of the child** test. This is the standard that courts use when determining child custody, or when reviewing the custody arrangements in a marriage settlement agreement. Note that it is not called the "best interests of the parents" test or the "he's a lousy bum and therefore shouldn't see his kids" test. What the judge wants to know is which arrangement will best serve this child, given her needs and the situation at hand. While the needs and desires of the parents are rightfully taken into consideration, it is the needs (and sometimes the desires) of the children that are paramount.

It is what the court concludes is in the child's best interests that determines how the possible permutations of the four custody possibilities pan out. Analyzing what is in the child's best interests is not always easy. Courts will look at a variety of factors:

- The age of the children
- The parents' parenting skills (An alcoholic, abusive, or drug-addicted parent is less likely to get physical custody. A loving, supportive parent is more likely to get custody.)

- The need for stability in a child's life (Parents who must travel for work, for example, are at a disadvantage.)
- The physical and mental health of both the kids and the parents
- The ability of the parent to give the child food, shelter, education, stability, love, and support
- The established patterns in the child's life
- The willingness of a parent to encourage the children to have a relationship with the other parent (Mature adults who understand that a child needs both a mother and a father are more likely to get custody.)
- The wishes of the child, when the child is of sufficient maturity to make good decisions (As a general, but by no means strict, rule, the desires of a child under the age of eleven will not likely be taken into account by a court.)

While none of the above factors alone is decisive, a combination that establishes the needs of the child and the ability of the parents to provide for those needs constitutes the child's best interests.

There are a few more important ingredients that may go into the custody mix. Parents who leave their mate for a gay or lesbian lover will likely find that the court may penalize them for this choice. Also, it is unconstitutional for a court to consider the race of a parent when making the custody determination.

HOW TO GET A COURT TO GRANT YOU PHYSICAL CUSTODY.
Custody disputes are an ugly reality in divorce. It is not uncommon for one parent to try to deny custody to the other in a sick game in which the children are the losers.

On the other hand, there are times when one parent has a legitimate reason to want sole physical custody. Either she believes the other spouse to be an unfit parent or she truly believes that the children would be best served in one home. If the parents cannot work out a suitable arrangement, then it will be up to the judge to decide where the children will live.

In order to win a custody battle, you need to prove two things. First, you need to prove to the court that you are the better parent—that you have the ability to better love, care for, and nourish the child; that you can give the child a good home and a stable environment; and that the child will still be able to have a good relationship with the other parent while in your home. Second, you need to prove that the child's best interests will be served by living in your home alone—that it would be too disruptive to go back and forth between two homes; that your child's educational and social needs would be best met in one home; and, in short, that the child would be happier in your home. Prove that and you should win.

The Important Legal Concept to Remember: "Custody" is both where the child will live (physical) and who will make the important decisions for the child (legal). Courts look at the best interests of the child, not the parents, when analyzing or reviewing custody arrangements.

17

ELEMENTS OF A SUCCESSFUL CUSTODY AGREEMENT

Beginning negotiations
Elements of a parenting agreement

BEGINNING NEGOTIATIONS. Understanding the four custody permutations discussed in the previous chapter should enable divorcing spouses to draft a custody agreement that works for everyone. An arrangement in which the interests of the children are paramount, a negotiation designed to allow both parents to "win," will be an agreement that proves to be stronger, and longer lasting, than a selfish one. That should be the goal.

There is another type of arrangement—a one-sided agreement that is usually negotiated by a spouse with more money and, therefore, more influence. This kind of agreement is a waste of time. One-sided agreements born of power foster anger and encourage the other side to breach the agreement. If there is ever a time to put hard feelings aside, to act magnanimously and be a big person, that time is now.

Sit down with your mate in a neutral place, with or without lawyers, and contemplate the future. What will life look like in a year? What do the kids need (keeping in mind that they need stability now above all else)? What arrangement can best meet those needs? These decisions are likely to be the most important you will make in your divorce. The discussions should not be rushed. When you become frustrated, as surely you will, always keep in mind that a court is waiting to make these decisions for you should you fail.

However, this process does not need to be done in a vacuum. It is always advisable to work closely with your attorney throughout the divorce. The custody talks can begin without attorneys, and then the lawyers can be brought in to draft any agreement made. Or the lawyers can be present the whole time. It depends on whatever is most comfortable.

Aside from attorneys, counselors and mediators are also available to assist in this process. A trained mediator's job is to help facilitate a settlement by acting as a neutral arbiter. For a complete discussion about mediation during divorce, see Chapter 20, "Mediation."

Once you and your spouse have decided upon a method of negotiation, be it alone, with lawyers, or with a mediator, the next step is to construct a parenting agreement. This agreement will hopefully, but not necessarily, become part of an overall marriage settlement agreement that will also include alimony, child support, and property division.

Christopher and Gwen were able to settle most of the issues that cropped up during their divorce. The stumbling block came when they could not agree on who would get physical custody of their four children. They submitted their marriage settlement agreement to the judge for approval, and the issue of custody was left for trial. After hearing the facts, the judge awarded sole physical custody to Gwen and legal custody was to be shared jointly. The judge gave Christopher visitation rights two weekends a month, and then modified the settlement agreement by making Christopher pay $1,000 in child support per month.

Christopher and Gwen really did nothing wrong. They agreed when they could, and took their chances when they could not, although Christopher probably could have negotiated a better deal for himself had he been less a risk taker.

ELEMENTS OF A PARENTING AGREEMENT. A good parenting agreement will do much more than spell out custody and enumerate visitation. There are scores of potential problems that may arise in the ensuing years, and the more the agreement anticipates and deals with these issues, the less likely there will be misunderstandings and future court dates.

A parenting arrangement should include the following:

1. *Delineation of custody:* The rest of the parenting agreement will flow from the decision as to who will get physical custody of the children. While physical custody should probably be given to one parent, the other parent should not be left out of raising the children. Parenting arrangements are often very creative, especially if the parents continue to live near each other.

   The kids could live with one parent all week and the other on weekends, or every other weekend. They could live with Dad most of the time, but see Mom every Wednesday for dinner, and live with her all summer. That some parents can get very creative is seen in the example of a mother in San Francisco. She lives with her kids and new husband on the bottom floor of a two-story flat. Her ex-husband lives *upstairs*. Mom has physical custody, but the kids see their dad all they want. While this may be difficult to fathom, it serves to illustrate that your living arrangement and custody agreement is limited only by your imagination.

   For those parents who do not anticipate getting along postdivorce, the best tip you can get is that it would be very wise to get physical custody and have the title "custodial parent." The parent who ends up with that designation is really the one in the driver's seat as far as the children are concerned. The kids will live with that parent and that parent will likely be receiving child support. Although the parenting agreement may make many provisions for the noncustodial parent, do not be misled—the custodial parent wields the power after a divorce.

Legal custody must also be part of the plan, but, as indicated, both parents usually have a say in the decisions affecting the child's upbringing.

2. *Visitation, holidays, vacations:* Custody and visitation go hand in hand—when one parent gets physical custody, the other gets visitation rights. Once it is decided where the children will live, visitation will follow. Chapter 19, "Visitation," deals exclusively with possible visitation arrangements.

Holidays such as Christmas are usually split evenly, with one parent getting the children one year, and the other the next year. Alternatively, the kids could be with their father every Christmas Eve, and with their mother every Christmas morning. It is a matter of personal preference. Other major holidays are usually split evenly, alternating years, as well—Thanksgiving, Easter, birthdays, etc. Mom should get the kids every Mother's Day and Dad should get them every Father's Day.

Like holidays, vacations (Christmas, Easter, and summer) also need to be divvied up. Parents often switch roles in the summer, with the noncustodial parent getting the kids all summer, save for maybe two weeks. Christmas vacation, usually two weeks long, can be split in half or alternated yearly. Again, it is a matter of preference.

As a word of caution, it is best to try to carry out any arrangement in a spirit of goodwill and cooperation. It is going to be very difficult raising a child with a person you are no longer married to. Although the custody agreement will set forth each parent's rights and responsibilities, life is rarely as neat as the agreement. Hopefully, the more flexibility you give your ex-spouse, the more you will get in return.

3. *Religion and education:* Critical decisions on these matters should not be left unresolved. If the parents are the same

religion, then there should be little conflict. If, however, the parents are of different religions, or if one is far more religious than the other, then the situation is ripe for strife. Be that as it may, it is important to set out if and how religious training is to be carried out, and by whom. Will the girl be confirmed? Will the boy go to church?

Education too should be included. If a child has special educational needs, this must be described, schools should be listed, and the agreement should state who will pay for the schooling. If private or home schooling is desired, this too needs to be specified.

4. *Insurance and medical:* The children's health-care provider should be mentioned, responsibility for payment of premiums must be decided, and possibly a specification as to who will take the kids to regular medical and dental checkups might be included.

5. *The possibility of a move:* If the custodial parent anticipates that he may have to move in the future, the agreement should take this into account. In all probability, if the spouses are living near each other, the noncustodial spouse will oppose this provision for good reason. If it can become part of the agreement, then when the time comes to leave, no one will be surprised. Related matters should also then be included: visitation times for the other spouse, allocation of payments for flying the children back and forth, and so on.

6. *Miscellaneous:* Other items that might be included are child-care arrangements and financial accountability; provisions allowing for foreign travel with a parent, but limiting the duration or countries of destination; a statement that neither parent can move the children out of the area without the express written consent of the other; or a statement that neither parent will interfere with the relationship between the children and the other parent.

For an example of how a custody agreement is incorporated into a marriage settlement agreement, see Chapter 22, "A Typical Marriage Settlement Agreement."

The Important Legal Concept to Remember: When deciding how to raise children after a divorce, draft an agreement that puts their interests above all else.

18

CUSTODY DISPUTES AND MODIFICATION

Custody disputes
Breaching the agreement
Moving with the children
Modification

Compare the following scenarios:

Danielle and Tony hated each other by the end of their marriage, and their divorce was worse. Although Danielle had sole physical custody of their daughter, Mara, the parenting arrangement gave Tony a lot of time with her. Danielle was determined to make Tony's life miserable, and she did. Tony finally became so exasperated at Danielle's constant irritability, inflexibility, and indecisiveness that he took a job in another state and did not tell Danielle. He moved there with Mara one weekend when Danielle was out of town. Danielle spent the next two years trying to find and see Mara again.

Danielle was sick of Tony, but knew that he was a good father. Despite herself, she made sure that Mara saw a lot of her father, even when it was her turn to have Mara. As the years went by, Tony began to appreciate Danielle's efforts. When the job opportunity in the neighboring state arose, he decided it was better for both him and Mara to stay near Danielle. He declined the offer.

CUSTODY DISPUTES. Any tool that the law can offer to resolve a custody dispute will be a poor substitute for an adult, good-working relationship between ex-spouses. Even the most carefully drafted, well-planned, good-faith parenting agreement will eventually result in a dispute. Happily married parents have disagreements about raising their kids, and unhappily divorced parents will as well—that's a fact. The issue is not *whether* you will fight with your ex-spouse about how to raise the kids, but *how* those disputes will be resolved.

Of course one party can go to court and get a parenting agreement enforced. Sure, the other parent can exert her rights as the custodial parent to thwart the intent of the parenting agreement. Neither method is desirable. Lawyers are expensive, courts are time-consuming. Unless the problem is truly serious, working it out or simply ignoring it are the best options.

Serious custody problems, on the other hand, usually require expert assistance to resolve. Moving away and not living up to the agreement are the most common of these types of disputes, and there is little else one can do other than going to mediation or back to court.

BREACHING THE AGREEMENT. A parent can violate the custody agreement in any number of ways: failing to see the kids or failing to return them when scheduled are two examples. When this occurs it is important to document the violation. Keep a journal of each incident in order to show a pattern of violation. It is this pattern that the court will want to see; an isolated event wastes the court's time and irritates judges.

Parents who repeatedly violate court orders are dealt with severely—fines and jail are distinct possibilities. You can bring a spouse who violates the court's custody order into line by initiating a contempt of court proceeding. Contempt of court means that one party has willfully violated the court's order and that criminal sanctions are appropriate. Contempt of court is in fact quasi-criminal in nature, and if found guilty, the violating spouse can be fined, sent to jail, or put on probation. It is a big legal stick that often stops repeat offenders.

MOVING WITH THE CHILDREN. What if you need or want to move legally, and you have custody of the kids? The noncustodial spouse can move without a problem. If she ends up far away from the children, it is her choice and her loss. The problem with a move by the custodial parent is that the noncustodial parent will likely oppose the move if it would result in less time for her to spend with the children. What is a custodial parent to do?

If the settlement agreement has a moving provision in it, then a move will be easier, but by no measure a sure thing. There is nothing to stop a noncustodial parent from challenging the move, even if the settlement agreement has a move-away clause. However, if the agreement does not have a move-away clause, and no resolution can be reached, then the parent who wants to challenge the move usually must bring the other parent back to court so that a judge can resolve the matter (although binding arbitration is another possible solution).

When a court challenge ensues, neither keeping the kids where they are nor allowing them to leave is a foregone conclusion. Not surprisingly, the court will look at the best interests of the children when evaluating such a possible move. The court will consider factors such as

- whether the children will be better off financially and educationally by the move;
- whether it is a necessity that the parent moves (a new job), or whether the move is being done out of spite or boredom;
- how the lives of the kids might be disrupted by the change;
- what the effect on the visitation with the noncustodial parent will be.

No court can stop you from moving. Interstate travel is a constitutional right. The court can, however, stop your children from going with you. Since this area of law is in great flux, an attorney should be consulted.

MODIFICATION. The court retains power (called jurisdiction) over a divorce, even after it is finalized. This allows the court to later adjudicate matters such as custody disputes and modification issues. However, custody modifications do not *have* to be done through the court. If the divorced spouses can agree to the proposed changes, they can then sign a document that modifies the existing settlement by agreement.

Jean and Adam shared custody of their daughter, Jill. By the time Jill was fifteen, she did not care that the agreement said she was to live in both homes. She was sick of the arrangement and wanted to live with her dad. Jean and Adam agreed, and also agreed that Adam should not pay child support to Jean any longer if Jill was living with him full-time. They signed a stipulation, modified their previous agreement, and had it signed by the judge.

When the parties cannot agree to the proposed modification, a request must be made to the court that sets forth the factual and legal reasons why the change is necessary. Getting a court to change visitation or custody is not an easy thing to do. A mere dislike for the present arrangement is insufficient.

Two things must be proved. First, the party who is requesting the change must show that there has been a change in circumstances necessitating the requested modification. The so-called change in circumstances test is a difficult one to pass. The change must be substantial. The effect must be significant. A custodial parent who begins drinking and neglecting the child would meet this test. A parent whose new boyfriend sleeps over a lot may not. A parent who starts abusing a child would pass muster, but a parent who occasionally swats the kid on the behind would not. A parent planning to leave the state might constitute changed circumstances, but a parent who wants to move to the next town would not.

A change in circumstances is not all that is needed. As with the original custody arrangement, it must also be proved that the requested modification will be in the child's best interests. This twofold test—change in circumstances and best interests of the child—requires that an important alteration has occurred in the life of the child that can be resolved only by altering the custody arrangement and modifying the original decision. This is not an easy task.

The Important Legal Concept to Remember: Custody arrangements are not easily modified, and a decision to breach an agreement because it is disliked may result in criminal sanctions. It is usually better for the divorced couple to work out custody disputes and modification issues themselves; "self-help" is too risky.

VISITATION

Visitation is the flip side of the custody coin. When a court grants physical custody of a child to a parent, it almost always simultaneously grants extensive rights of visitation to the other parent. These visitation rights are not to be taken lightly; just as custody carries the weight of a legal court order, so too does visitation. And, just as with interference with custody by the non-custodial parent, interference with visitation by the custodial parent (which is probably more common) constitutes contempt of court and therefore is criminal in nature.

TYPES OF VISITATION. There are two types of possible visitation arrangements—unstructured and structured. An unstructured visitation arrangement is called **reasonable visitation**. This arrangement leaves it up to the divorcing adults to work out a suitable plan. For example:

> Bob and Wanda divorced on fairly good terms (as well as could be expected) and agreed that their kids should live with Wanda and that Bob would get reasonable visitation. Although they began by allowing visitation every weekend,

as time evolved, Bob and Wanda found that it worked best to allow Bob to see the kids every Wednesday evening, every other weekend, and all summer. This arrangement lasted for eight years, until all the kids were adults.

The real advantage of this type of arrangement is that it allows the adults to behave like adults and work things out. The risk is that *reasonable* is one of those wishy-washy legal words subject to whatever interpretation a party might give it. And if the two people involved could not agree enough to make their relationship work, the real danger is that they would be equally unable to make their "reasonable" visitation arrangement work.

That is why the other option, of structured visitation, is probably in everyone's best interests. Structured visitation is usually called a **fixed visitation schedule**. Under this plan, fixed times and days are built into the visitation schedule. The arrangement is usually very detailed, setting forth exactly which days, including the time of day, the noncustodial parent will be with the child. It should also state which parent will pick up the child and which will drop her off. It should set forth which holidays the noncustodial visitation parent will get. Yet while it should detail enough to give everyone an idea of exactly what to expect, it should not be so fixed that there is no room for some flexibility, with regard to either weekly visits or holidays.

RIGHTS OF NONCUSTODIAL PARENTS. Whatever plan is chosen, keep in mind that visitation is a right that is *not dependent* upon custody or alimony payments. For example, if a husband is continually late, or in arrears, in his support payments, the wife cannot unilaterally punish him by preventing him from seeing his children. By the same token, if the wife interferes with the husband's visitation, it is illegal for the husband to stop all scheduled payments. **Self-help** methods such as these are as illegal as not paying child support. The appropriate resolution is to take the husband who does not pay, or the wife who inter-feres, back to court.

Also, you cannot force a parent to use the visitation given to him by the court. If a parent refuses to see his kids, it's his loss, and there is nothing anyone can do about it, not even a judge. Continual refusal to utilize visitation can, however, be used to get an increase in child support since child support payments are partially based on the percentage of time each parent spends with the child. (See Chapter 25, "Violation and Modification.")

RESTRICTED VISITATION. It is when a parent has a proven his-tory of abuse or neglect that a court is likely to restrict visitation and order supervised visits. Unsubstantiated fears and allega-tions will not do. There must be a legitimate fear that the spouse is an unqualified parent and is therefore a danger to the children.

If that is the case, the court will likely order supervised visi-tation, and, even then, possibly only for a limited time. The supervising adult will be present for all visits and could be a clergy member, friend, or court-appointed independent party. In very rare instances, when the parent has proven himself to be a threat to the child, the court may deny visitation altogether.

Yet the question remains, what is in the best interests of the child? The law believes that a child needs frequent and contin-uous contact with both parents. Obviously, there can be little bonding or positive interaction between a parent and child with a third party present. For that reason, restricted visits are rare, and are ordered only when there is a substantial chance that the parent is an immediate threat to the welfare of his child.

VISITS BY GRANDPARENTS. Grandparents have rights too. They have independent relationships with their grandchildren, which some states recognize. First among those rights is the right to visit with their grandchildren. While the law usually recognizes these rights, parents sometimes do not, and the grandparents may have to go to court to get those rights enforced.

The Important Legal Concept to Remember: The rights of noncustodial parents to visit their children are as important, and as legally protected, as the rights of custodial parents.

ENDING THE CASE

MEDIATION

Claire and Stephen were tired. They were tired of fighting, tired of each other, and tired of their marriage. Although Claire was happy when Stephen finally served her with divorce papers, she vowed not to go quietly. They had too much money and too many assets for her simply to walk away. She hired the best attorney in town, paid the $10,000 retainer, and told her lawyer, "Get him!"

MEDIATION IN GENERAL. Striking a compromise, backing down, and not getting everything you want are the hallmarks of a negotiated settlement agreement. However, considering the alternatives, it is not such a bad deal. Litigation is an adversarial win/lose process. Settlements should be a win/win process in which both parties are reasonably satisfied that the outcome met their needs and that they struck a deal everyone can live with.

Settlements can occur in a variety of ways. They can be a result of informal chats with a spouse, structured settlement negotiations with attorneys, or a result of mediation. In many states, mediation is often ordered by the court prior to trial.

Mediation is a nonadversarial process that attempts to bridge gaps, find common ground, and resolve differences. Mediators are neutral third parties whose job it is to assist the parties in creating an agreement that works for everybody. And, while permissible, attorneys need not be present.

Mediation is often confused with arbitration. It should not be since they are quite different. Arbitration is almost a minitrial. The arbitrator acts as a judge, hears the evidence, and renders a decision. Like a judge, the arbitrator's decision is usually binding and final. The only differences between a trial and an arbitration are that arbitration is quicker, less expensive, and a bit less formal. Arbitration is not recommended for divorce cases precisely because it is so much like a trial. The adversarial litigation system that mediation attempts to circumvent prevails at an arbitration.

THE ADVANTAGES OF MEDIATION. Mediation, on the other hand, has true advantages. First, it is a flexible process that can be used as extensively as needed. It can be used to settle major wars or minor skirmishes. Ideally, the mediation settlement will allow the parents and children to see each other, will provide for reasonable financial commitments, and will divide the property and debts equitably. An agreement that everyone can live with is an agreement that will be followed.

Mediation is also a confidential process. Whatever is said to the mediator is kept private, and whatever results are reached (good or bad) also remain confidential, unless the couple submits the agreement reached to the court for approval. That is the final advantage. If the process works, the parties can submit the agreement for court approval; if not, then not.

One year, five depositions, and $20,000 later, Claire was no closer to getting her desired divorce than the day she began. Exasperated, she swallowed her pride, called Stephen, and asked, "Do you want to go to mediation to see if we can split up the assets?" Stephen was only too happy to agree.

THE PROCESS. Mediation can indeed often be a decision born of desperation. After months or years of litigation, spouses often find that the adversarial course they have been on is fruitless and expensive. They want to resolve the issues and get on with their lives, but they do not know how to without looking weak.

Attorneys almost invariably know good mediators, or one can be found by calling the local bar association, going to the courthouse, or looking in the Yellow Pages. The main thing to look for in a mediator is someone who has had extensive experience in divorce cases, and someone whom neither party knows. The mediator must be neutral and independent for the process to work.

After finding a mediator, a mutually acceptable time for the mediation will be set. The mediation may take an hour, a day, or several days—once the issues involved are made clear to the mediator, he or she can estimate how many sessions will be needed.

Most mediations will proceed something like this: at the scheduled time and date, the mediator will likely bring both parties, and their attorneys, if they are invited, into one room for an opening session. If the spouses are so acrimonious that they make such a meeting pointless, they will probably start in different rooms. Either way, this beginning session serves the dual purposes of allowing both parties to give their points of view about the situation while concurrently providing the mediator with necessary background information.

The mediator will probably next put each party in a separate room and continue the process by conducting a type of "shuttle diplomacy," whereby he goes back and forth between the rooms, making offers and counteroffers, prodding, cajoling, pulling, and sometimes yanking the parties toward a settlement.

Like negotiations, a mediation can take on a life all its own. The parties become tired, the mediator gets anxious, and a need to settle permeates the process. While the mediator will do almost anything within the bounds of ethics to get the parties to agree to a settlement, do not be fooled by the mediator's tactics. In one session he may act as your friend, in another, your adversary. He is surely doing the same thing in the other room. It is all designed to coax an agreement out of two people who dislike and distrust each other.

> After eight hours of arduous negotiations, the mediator had just about given up on Stephen and Claire. Although they had resolved many of their differences that day, a few remained. The mediator went to Claire and stated, "If you leave here today, you can forget ever settling this case with Stephen. He's tired and angry. You need to compromise. Let me ask you this, what will happen if you don't settle today?" Claire knew that another six months of fighting, culminating in a trial, could break her financially and emotionally. She agreed to settle, and finally cut a deal.

If successful, the parties will agree to resolve most or all of their differences, compromise, and end their case. It should be a great relief. The mediator will draft an outline of the major points agreed to, which the attorneys will later put in legal language. That agreement can then become all or part of the final divorce decree, submitted to the judge for approval.

The Important Legal Concept to Remember: Mediation is a relatively inexpensive and usually a highly effective way to end a divorce.

21

HOW TO NEGOTIATE A GREAT DEAL

Mediation is only one type of negotiation that you may find yourself in along the bumpy path to divorce. Whether negotiating a settlement yourself or with the assistance of an attorney, divorce ensures that you will be negotiating aplenty.

Negotiating is something people do every day, although they may not realize it. Whether it is getting the cable company to come before noon or asking for a raise, you are constantly negotiating. The same is true in your divorce. Cutting a deal with your attorney, choosing a time for your deposition, or bluffing regarding a possible sale of the house are all forms of negotiation. Dividing property and dealing with child custody matters can be among the most arduous negotiations you will ever encounter. However, if you follow the six rules outlined below, you are apt to get a pretty good deal.

Rule 1. *Never, never, make the first offer:* This is Rule 1 for a reason. Consider this scenario:

> Spencer and Susie agreed to try to settle their alimony dispute. Spencer made a lot more money than Susie, and he also had a separate trust fund. Because she had caught him with a lover, and because he did not want word of that to get out, Spencer was prepared to buy Susie off if need be.

At the negotiating session, Spencer forced Susie to make the first offer by asking, "What do you need to live on, Susie?" Not wanting to alienate Spencer too much, Susie answered, "One thousand dollars a month." Spencer agreed, and papers were drawn up. What Susie did not know was that Spencer was prepared to pay her $2,500 a month if he had to.

Although Susie had no idea what Spencer was prepared or able to pay, look at what might have happened had Susie followed Rule 1 and simply *refused* to make the first offer:

After Spencer asked Susie how much she needed to live on, Susie (thinking about Rule 1) answered, "I have no idea how much you can afford, Spencer. What would you consider a reasonable price?" Susie thereby forced Spencer to make the first offer. Spencer thought about it, knew his budget allowed $2,500, and answered $2,000. Susie agreed.

By refusing to make the first offer, Susie made an extra $1,000 a month.

By the same token, when you make the first offer, you are telling the other side what your minimum bid is. Even though Susie would have been happy with $1,000, by forcing Spencer to make the first offer, she found out that Spencer's minimum was $2,000.

Sometimes the other side knows Rule 1 and simply refuses to make the first offer. What then? In that case, you are allowed to make the first offer, but make it outrageous.

Spencer refused to make Susie an offer, and kept insisting that she offer first. Finally, Susie said, "Okay Spence, I want ten thousand dollars a month." Spencer laughed, and countered with $2,000. Susie, wary of Rule 2, countered back. "Five thousand dollars," she said. "Three thousand," said Spencer. "Thirty-five hundred," countered Susie. "Deal," Spencer concluded.

Rule 2. *Never accept the first offer:* People enter negotiations knowing that they will have to either go up or come down from their starting point. That is the essence of good negotiations. There is nothing to "negotiate" if one side refuses to compromise. An experienced negotiator will always begin the process, depending upon her position, with a high or low figure. You should too. Always enter a negotiation with a number higher or lower (depending upon your position) than where you want to end up. Build some fudging room into your position.

> Tired of dealing with Susie, Spencer took a trip to New York. While there, he planned to go see the Knicks play. Unfortunately, the game he had wanted to see was sold out. He went to Madison Square Garden on the evening of the game anyway, put $50 in one pocket, $50 in another pocket, and kept another $10 in his wallet. Thirty minutes before the game, a scalper was willing to sell Spencer a ticket for $100. Spencer declined, knowing Rule 2. Five minutes before the game, Spencer offered $50. The scalper knew Rule 2 too, and countered with $75. Spencer took the $50 out of one pocket and said, "This is all I have." "Seventy-five dollars," said the scalper. Spencer opened his wallet, showed it to the scalper, and said, "Sixty dollars is it." The scalper took the money, Spencer saw his game, and he had $50 left over.

Even though Spencer was willing to spend another $50 for a seat, he did not have to because he followed Rule 2. He knew that the scalper's price was a "highball" figure, as most first offers are. Spencer also knew that if he waited until the game was to begin he could get the ticket for less than $100 because at that point the scalper would start to get desperate.

Rule 3. *Know your bottom line:* Never enter a negotiation without having figured out exactly what you want *beforehand*. Have a bottom line in mind that you are committed to, and do not waver. A negotiating session can take on a life and momentum all its own that is too easy to get swept up into.

After Spencer got back from New York, he and Susie decided to try to negotiate a property settlement since the alimony session had gone so well. Together they owned a house, two cars, some stock, and a mountain cabin. Susie really wanted the house. Spencer wanted the house too.

The negotiations went on for hours, and every possible combination of property division was considered. After ten hours, Spencer bluffed and said, "This is my last offer. You get the cabin and a car. No more." Susie was exhausted, the attorneys were costing a fortune, and everyone wanted to go home. She agreed.

Susie was too tired to remember Rule 3. What Susie really wanted was the house. But because she was so tired, and because the session had taken on a momentum all its own, she forgot to stick to her bottom line. Had she walked away and remembered her bottom line, she may have ended up with the house.

Rule 4. *Use some tricks now and then:* Every good negotiator has some tricks up her sleeve that enable her to bluff the other side when need be. There are several that you can use to gain an advantage.

· *Good-cop/bad-cop:* A very good, well-known trick is the good-cop/bad-cop routine. In order to use it, there must be two negotiating partners—two lawyers, a lawyer and a client, it does not really matter. In order to utilize this trick, prior to the negotiating session the two people need to confer and agree on their designated roles. One person takes on the nice-guy/reasonable-person/good-cop role, and the other takes on the jerk/unreasonable-person/bad-cop role.

Once negotiations begin, the jerk acts like a jerk. He or she makes unreasonable demands, gets angry, maybe even storms out of the negotiations. Then, in full view of the opposing side, the nice guy tries to talk some sense into the jerk. Once that happens, the nice guy is immediately and forever looked upon as honest and trustworthy. From then on, any offer or counteroffer the good-cop/nice-guy makes is assumed to be reasonable, even if it is patently unreasonable.

· *The bluff*: One way to get what you want is to pretend you do not want it—that you want something else instead. That thing instead is called a red herring. For example, if you are negotiating with your husband and you want the dining room set, ask instead for the bedroom set that you know he likes. Act like you really want that bedroom set. After bartering for a while, sigh and say, "Okay, you can have the bedroom set. I'll take the dining room set." The advantage of this trick is that you get to look reasonable *and* you get what you want. The risk, of course, is that you may end up with a bedroom set.

> Spencer knew that Susie really wanted the house and the stock. He really wanted the cabin and the stock. For the two months that they dickered about their property, Spencer kept insisting that he get the house. Finally, one day he said, "I am so tired of fighting about this. I'll take the cabin, I guess. You can have the house, but you have to throw in the stock." Susie was thrilled, and she agreed.

· *The intense reaction*: This trick is a variation on the bluff. When the other side makes an offer or a proposal that is unacceptable, try to react in one of these ways and see if he does not back down a little:

SILENCE: When your husband demands that you buy him out of the house, instead of selling it and splitting the profits, sit there in stone-cold silence. Do not say a word! The next thing out of his mouth, if you allow him to speak next, should be a more reasonable offer.

OUTRAGE: Outrage is useful when things are stuck or when you are not being taken seriously. It works to get the message across that you are not to be fooled with. Blow up! Be a jerk! And then cool down, even apologize. Most people do not like conflict, and the opposition will be much more careful in what they offer from then on, knowing what a hothead you are.

> Susie took the money Spencer paid her and went to buy a new car. When she got to the used car lot, she found a red sports car she loved. The salesman told her the price was $10,000. Susie stared at him in shocked silence for five seconds, turned on her heels, and headed back to her car. "Whoa, slow down, little lady!" he exclaimed. "How does nine thousand sound?"

Rule 5. *Have a credible threat if negotiations fail:* A key element of most successful negotiations is fear. You must create in the opponent a realistic fear that there will be negative consequences if the deal falls through. If an opponent has nothing to lose if negotiations fail, then there is little incentive to negotiate in good faith. If the car salesman does not fear that you will walk off the lot without his car, he has no reason to lower his price. If the general manager does not think you will sign with another team, he won't raise his offer.

In a divorce negotiation, the best threat is that you will take the case all the way through trial if you do not get a good deal. Since trial is a very expensive, very risky proposition, the fear of trial should force your spouse to negotiate honestly. The threat must be fairly realistic to work, though. If your husband knows that you cannot afford to go to trial, your threat to do so would be hollow. You must either be a good actor or really be willing to follow through with your threat for this tactic to work.

Rule 6. *Try to create a win-win outcome:* As indicated, there are basically two types of deals. The first is where one party wins and the other loses; the other is where both parties feel that they won. It is the second type of deal that one should strive for.

Now, this may seem to conflict with some of the tricks explained above, but it really does not. The strategies above are used to create an advantage when needed, and usually can accelerate a stalled negotiation. They are not intended to be used as consistent hardball tactics because such a strategy inevitably fails. Getting every possible thing you want is not only unlikely—it is inadvisable.

Hardball negotiators who attempt to win at all costs often end up with one of two outcomes, neither positive. First, they may end up with nothing. Hardball negotiations usually create such hard feelings that the other side may refuse to cut a deal just on principal. Second, if they do get a deal, it is apt to be so one-sided as to be unworkable. The only thing worse than no deal is a deal that the other side cannot possibly live up to. What happens when a husband, tired of fighting, agrees to pay his estranged wife $1,500 a month when all he brings home is $2,500? He will make a few payments, realize that he cannot possibly live up to the agreement, and quit paying. Both sides will end up with nothing more than an unworkable agreement and a lot of legal bills.

A negotiation that was tough but fair has a far higher likelihood of resulting in a good deal than any mean-spirited interaction. Fight hard, fight fair, be willing to compromise, and be committed to getting a deal done. If both sides are moderately happy (and, therefore, moderately unhappy), they probably have the best deal they can hope for.

The Important Legal Concept to Remember: Good negotiators are made, not born. By studying the six rules listed above, anyone can negotiate a great deal.

22

A TYPICAL MARRIAGE
SETTLEMENT AGREEMENT

If you are attempting to settle your case, then by the end of the divorce you will need to have come to an agreement with your spouse on property and debt division, child custody and visitation matters, and spousal and child support. In order to have legal, binding effect, the agreement must take the form of a stipulated marriage settlement agreement. What follows is a typical agreement that may be used as a prototype.

A caveat: remember that each state has different laws and guidelines. While this settlement agreement generally covers all important issues, the specifics may turn out differently in different states. For example, California has a very rigid formula for child support. This is not true in all states.

Marty and Sandy were married for seventeen years. During the course of their marriage they had two beautiful sons. Marty worked full-time as a carpet salesman, and Sandy worked part-time running her housekeeping business. At the time of their divorce, their house was worth $200,000, and they owed $150,000 on it. They owned three cars, and they also had an antique collection worth $25,000. Sandy's housekeeping business was valued at $20,000, and Marty had a pension worth $30,000 through his job. Their debts totaled $20,500.

Both were loving parents. They realized early on that it would be best to avoid dragging their kids to court. After four months, they agreed on the following:

MARRIAGE SETTLEMENT AGREEMENT

I. RECITALS

[Notice how this section sets forth the parties, their children, and other pertinent information.]

Pursuant to the laws of the state of Washington, this agreement is made by and entered into between SANDRA BODIAN MARCUS ("Wife" or "Mother") and MARTIN LESTER MARCUS ("Husband" or "Father") on the date stated below.

The parties were legally married in Seattle, Washington, on September 11, 1980. There are two minor children of this marriage: LARRY ALAN MARCUS, born August 13, 1983, and PAUL STEVEN MARCUS, born April 30, 1986.

Irreconcilable differences have arisen between the parties *[this means that this is a no-fault divorce]* which have led to the immediate breakdown of their marital relationship, and therefore the parties separated on December 22, 1997.

The parties now intend, by this agreement, to make a final and complete settlement of all matters between them arising out of their marriage, including, but not limited to, child custody and support, alimony, and property and debt division. *[Marty and Sandy left nothing to chance. They worked out all their differences and the settlement agreement will cover all outstanding issues from their marriage.]*

In consideration of these facts and circumstances, Husband and Wife agree as follows:

II. S EPARATION

The parties shall live separately and apart from each other, and each shall be free to do as he or she wishes without control or direction from the other, except as set forth in this agreement.

III. CHILD CUSTODY AND VISITATION

1. *Physical Custody:* The Mother shall have primary physical custody of both minor children. The children shall stay with the Mother each and every day and night, except as outlined below in sections 4 and 5.

2. *Legal Custody:* The Husband and Wife shall jointly share legal custody of both minor children. Both parties agree to consult with the other prior to making any important decisions regarding the children. The parties agree to raise the children in the Catholic faith. *[Like many couples, Marty and Sandy agreed that having one primary residence would be in the best interests of their children, but that both parents should be very involved in raising the kids.]*

3. *Successor Custodian:* The Wife agrees that in the event of her death prior to either child reaching the age of eighteen years, the Husband shall be named the custodial parent.

4. *Visitation:* The Father shall have reasonable visitation with the children at all times, as agreed upon by the parties. The parties will make every reasonable effort to accommodate the wishes of each other to ensure that the children have continuous contact with both parents.

5. *Specific Visitation:* The father shall have specific visitation rights which shall be as follows:

   A. The children shall stay with the Father every other weekend from Friday after school until the following Monday morning, when the Father will be responsible for getting the children to school. *[There is no room for misunderstanding.]*

   B. The children will be with the Father every Wednesday evening for dinner, and shall be returned to the Mother's house no later than 8:30 P.M. that evening.

   C. The children will be with the Father every Father's Day, and will be with the Mother every Mother's Day.

D. The children will spend one week of Christmas vacation with their Mother, and one week with their Father. Christmas Day and Christmas Eve shall alternate yearly between the parents, with the transfer of the children occurring at 10:00 A.M. Christmas Day each and every year. Beginning this year, the children will be with the Mother for the first week of vacation, and for Christmas Eve.

E. Thanksgiving holidays shall alternate yearly, with both children staying with one parent one year, and both with the other parent the next year. The children will be with the Father this year. *[Having one child in each home every year would be ludicrous.]*

F. Easter vacation (spring break) shall alternate yearly, beginning this year with the Mother.

G. Birthdays for the children shall alternate yearly. Each parent will have both children for birthdays one year, and the other parent will have both the next year, beginning this year with the Father.

H. Both sets of grandparents shall have reasonable visitation rights with the children, to be coordinated through the parents. Neither parent shall interfere with the children's visitation with the other set of grandparents. *[This way, everyone is protected.]*

[Marty and Sandy incorporated the idea of both scheduled and unscheduled visitation. They obviously intend to try to work together and allow Marty as much time with the boys as possible.]

6. *Misc.:* Both parents will share transportation expenses for vacations and holidays. Neither parent shall conceal or take the children out of the state of Washington without the prior written approval of the other parent.

IV. CHILD AND SPOUSAL SUPPORT

1. *Child Support:* Husband and Wife are informed of their rights and responsibilities under the laws of the state of Washing-

ton. Husband agrees to pay Wife $250 per month per child (presently $500 per month). Payments will begin the immediate month after this agreement is signed, and shall be due by the fifth day of each month. Said payments will continue until each child becomes self-supporting, reaches the age of nineteen, reaches the age of eighteen and is no longer a full-time high school student, or dies, whichever comes first.

Husband and Wife understand that there may be guidelines which differ from the amount stated above. They declare that even if this is so, this agreement is in the best interests of their children, and the needs of the children will be adequately met by this amount. *[Remember that each state has very different laws regarding child support. Check with an attorney before setting an amount different from the figure dictated by your state.]*

2. *Insurance:* The Husband shall have medical insurance for both children throughout the duration of his support obligation. Expenses not covered by insurance shall be borne equally by Husband and Wife.

3. *College:* Husband and Wife agree that all expenses for college for both children shall be paid two-thirds by the Father and one-third by the Mother, unless the Mother is working full-time by that time, in which case college expenses will be borne equally. *[Because Sandy was obviously so reasonable when it came to visitation (evidenced by the flexible agreement above) Marty was willing to take on more of the financial responsibility for the children.]*

4. *Spousal Support [Note that there are a variety of possible options here. The receiving party can waive support in exchange for other property, payments can be for a specific amount of time, or it can be paid indefinitely. It all depends upon the circumstances]:* In consideration of the terms and obligations outlined in this agreement, Husband agrees to pay Wife $250 per month, payable on the fifth day of each month, commencing the

month immediately following the signing of this agreement. Said payments will continue for five years and no longer. This termination date is final and absolute, and this term is not subject to modification. This paragraph specifically divests the parties from the ability, and the jurisdiction of this court, to alter this date. *[Sandy cannot go back to court and try to get her spousal support increased.]*

The parties agree that should Wife remarry, or should she go to court in an attempt to increase the amount of spousal support, all further spousal support obligations shall cease, and Husband will be obligated to make no further spousal support payments. *[This paragraph ensures that Sandy will not try to get more money.]*

The parties further agree that should Husband, at any time, become ninety days past due on either his child or spousal support obligations, he will owe wife an additional $100 per day for every day said payments are over ninety days late. *[This paragraph ensures that Marty will not be late with his payments.]*

Both Husband and Wife are aware that the conditions set forth in this spousal support section may result in hardship in the future. Both parties agree that this is their intent, and, by signing below, voluntarily and knowingly waive their right to contest this section or the conditions set forth herein.

V. DIVISION OF DEBTS

1. *Debts:* The debts listed below are either Husband's (H), Wife's (W), or joint (J). The responsible party shall be solely obligated to pay the debt in full, and shall hold harmless [hold harmless *is a legal term meaning that one party cannot legally go after the other party to pay the obligation]* the other party. The responsible party agrees to notify each creditor of the assumption of the obligation.

CREDITOR	AMOUNT	OBLIGATION OF H, W, OR J	RESPONSIBLE PARTY
Visa	$5,000	J	H
Visa	3,500	J	W
Household bills	2,000	J	W
Student loan	5,000	H	H
Business expenses	5,000	W	W·

[Even though Sandy accepted $500 more debt than Marty, it is made up in the next section, where she gets more property than he does. Notice that separate debts remained separate. Remember too that there is no guarantee that a party who agrees to pay a debt in the settlement agreement will in fact pay it. Settlement agreements are not binding on anyone but those who sign them. Visa does not really care if Marty agreed to pay the debt. If he fails to pay it, Visa will go after Sandy.]

2. *Taxes:* Husband and Wife have a tax liability for the year 1990 in the amount of $800. The parties have agreed to pay the cost of this liability evenly.

   Each parent may claim the tax exemption for one child in any tax year. *[The tax exemption for children is a very valuable bargaining chip.]*

VI. DIVISION OF PROPERTY

1. *Separate Property:*
   A. *Wife's Separate Property:* The following property is the sole and separate property of the Wife, and Husband forever waives and relinquishes any right or claim to this property:
      1. China set
      2. Antique rocking chair
      3. Miniature doll collection

B. *Husband's Separate Property:* The following property is the sole and separate property of the Husband, and Wife forever waives and relinquishes any right or claim to this property:

1. Craftsman tool set

2. 1957 T-bird automobile

3. Collected works of Ernest Hemingway

2. *Community Property [or jointly held property in noncommunity property states]:*

A. *Real Estate:* Husband and Wife are joint owners of real property located at 1800 Mariposa Lane, Seattle, Washington. The parties agree that title to the residence shall be placed in the name of the Husband and that he shall assume all debts associated with it, including, but not limited to, payment of all mortgages, encumbrances, taxes, insurance, and all other assessments. *[Marty ended up with the house.]*

Within thirty days of the signing of this document, Wife will sign a quitclaim deed conveying to Husband all of her right, title, and interest in the subject property. Should Wife fail to so convey the property, this agreement shall be, and shall constitute and operate, as such a conveyance. In such an event, the county auditor and recorder are authorized to transfer and record the same. *[This section protects Marty. If Sandy, for whatever reason, decides not to sign the deed, the settlement agreement can be used as the deed instead.]*

Concurrent with that transfer, and conditioned thereon, Husband will execute a note payable to Wife in the amount of $25,250. *[A note is similar to a check—Marty is promising to pay Sandy $25,250.]* The note will be due and payable three months after the date of the transfer. *[Sandy can cash the check in three months.]* Should Wife so request it, the note will be secured by a mortgage on the property. *[If the check bounces, the mortgage would* *grant Sandy the ability to sell the house in order to get paid.]*

[Marty and Sandy had a few options with regard to the house. They could have sold it altogether, or given it (and the debt) to Marty in exchange for the antiques going to Sandy. However, Sandy needed money, so she insisted upon the provision above whereby Marty buys her out of the house. Her 50 percent of the equity is worth $25,000. The other $250 makes up for the extra debt she took on in the debt division section. Marty will need to refinance the house in order to pay off the note, or get the money to pay her some other way.]

B. *Automobiles:* Husband shall get possession of and title to the 1988 Camaro. Wife shall get possession of and title to the 1986 Chrysler minivan. The parties shall execute all title transfer documents necessary to effectuate this section. *[The third car was Marty's separate property, and was returned to him in that section.]*

C. *Bank Accounts:* All jointly held bank accounts will be closed. All separate accounts shall remain the sole and separate property of the party holding title thereto, and the other party forever waives and relinquishes any claim or right they have, or may have had, to the property.

D. *Household Goods:* All household goods, including appliances, furniture (excluding all antiques), and clothes have already been divided by the parties to their mutual satisfaction. All such property, whether acquired before or during marriage, shall remain the sole and separate property of that party in whose possession it now is. Both parties forever waive any claims or rights to the other's property. *[Marty and Sandy divided the household goods when Sandy moved out. They exchanged a few items before it was all over, and each now agrees that what they have is all they will get.]*

E. *Antiques:* All antiques collected by the parties while married will become the sole and separate property of the Wife upon the signing of this agreement, except as follows: Husband will receive the Wurlitzer jukebox, which the parties stipulate [*agree*] is worth $5,000. Wife forever waives any claims or rights to this property, and Husband forever waives any claims or rights to all other antique property.

F. *Pension Plan:* After full disclosure of the nature and extent of the vested pension plan of the Husband, and acceptance of each party that said pension plan is subject to division as marital property *[this means that both parties are aware of the fact that Sandy has an interest in Marty's pension]*, the parties have agreed to divide the plan as follows: Husband will retain and receive 100 percent of the plan, and Wife forever waives and relinquishes any claim or right she has, or may have had, in the plan.

[Again, there were a few things that Marty and Sandy could have done here. They could have split the antiques evenly, and the pension plan too. Or they could have sold all antiques, split the money, and split the pension. Instead, because they wanted to be free of each other, they decided that each would keep one of the assets.]

G. *Business:* After full disclosure of the extent of the Wife's housekeeping business, and acceptance of each party that said business is subject to division as marital property *[this means that both parties are aware of the fact that Marty has an interest in Sandy's business]*, the parties have agreed to divide the business as follows: Wife will retain 100 percent of the business, and Husband forever waives and relinquishes any claim or right he has, or may have had, in the business or its profits. *[The business is 100 percent Sandy's, and the pension is 100 percent Marty's.]*

[Notice how Marty and Sandy divided their major assets. They split the equity in the house ($25,000 each), and they split evenly the cars and household furniture without much fuss. Sandy kept her business, Marty kept his pension. Sandy got most of the antiques, although they used the $5,000 jukebox to even out the

deal for Marty. While neither got everything he or she wanted, both got most of what they wanted.]

VII. MISCELLANEOUS

[Do not be fooled by the title of this section. The following clauses are important to a fair and enforceable settlement agreement.]

1. *Future Debts:* Husband and Wife promise not to incur any debt or obligation for which the other may be held liable. Each agrees to indemnify and hold harmless the other in the event that a creditor brings a claim against one for the postsigning debts of the other. *[If Sandy takes on debt that Marty later becomes liable for, she promises to reimburse him for his share, and vice versa.]*

2. *Future Bankruptcy:* Within three years after the signing of this agreement, if either party elects to file for bankruptcy, he or she is obliged to notify the other party twenty-one days prior to said filing. The party being notified shall have the right to participate in that proceeding via consolidated case management. *[Many of the debts Marty and Sandy divided are joint debts, and a bankruptcy unfortunately often follows a divorce. If Marty files for bankruptcy, the creditors can legally go after Sandy for payment, and vice versa. A consolidated bankruptcy avoids this possibility.]*

3. *Attorney's Fees:* Both parties shall be responsible for their own attorney's fees. In the event that legal action is necessary to enforce the terms of this agreement, the parties agree that the party found in breach shall pay all attorney's fees and costs for both sides associated with that enforcement action.

4. *Entire Agreement:* Both parties agree that they are entering into this agreement voluntarily, and have had the opportunity to have this agreement reviewed by the attorney of their choice. Each party fully understands all terms of this agreement, and this agreement constitutes the full and entire agreement between the parties. Any previous oral or writ-

ten agreements are null and void, and the parties certify that this agreement is the final and complete settlement of all issues between the parties. *[This agreement is it; there are no other arrangements, oral or written. And even if there were, a court would look at this clause and decide that any other agreement between these parties would be unenforceable.]*

5. *Performance of Necessary Acts:* Each party shall take all actions necessary, and execute all instruments, deeds, forms, title transfer documents, and conveyances needed, to effectuate the terms of this agreement. Should either party fail to execute and deliver any necessary document, this agreement shall operate and constitute as such a properly executed instrument. All public and/or private officials are hereby authorized to accept this agreement in lieu of the necessary document usually needed for transfer. *[If Sandy fails to execute the quitclaim deed, this agreement will work in its place.]*

6. *Honest Representation:* Both parties warrant that they have made a full and complete disclosure of all finances, assets, and liabilities, including all pensions, profits, and incomes.

7. *Effective Date:* This agreement shall be effective upon approval by the court overseeing the dissolution of this marriage.

8. *Modification:* The parties agree that the court shall retain jurisdiction over this case to make whatever orders and modifications deemed necessary to carry out the will of the parties and the court. This agreement can be modified only in a writing signed by both parties. *[Only certain aspects of a marriage settlement can be modified: child custody and support, visitation, and spousal support. Everything else agreed to (e.g., division of debts) is not subject to modification. In Marty and Sandy's agreement, spousal support too is nonmodifiable since that section specifically forbids modification.]*

9. *Applicable Law:* The provisions of this agreement shall be construed and enforced in accordance with the laws of the state of Washington.

10. *Release of Liability:* Both parties, by affixing their signatures below, hereby release forever any and all claims they may have against each other. *[This agreement settles all outstanding issues between Marty and Sandy, and neither can sue the other for any related claims.]*

11. *Binding Effect:* All terms and conditions of this agreement, in whole or part, are expressly made binding upon all heirs, assigns, executors, administrators, personal representatives, and successors of the parties hereto.

12. *Cooperation:* This agreement is to be carried out in the spirit of goodwill and cooperation.

DATED _____   _____
                                  MARTY MARCUS

DATED _____   _____
                                  SANDY MARCUS

APPROVED AS TO FORM AND CONTENT:

DATED _____   _____
                                  ATTORNEY FOR MARTY MARCUS

DATED _____   _____
                                  ATTORNEY FOR SANDY MARCUS

IT IS SO ORDERED:

DATED _____   _____
                                  JUDGE OF THE SUPERIOR COURT

23

TRIAL

Elements of a trial
How to make a good witness
Appeal

ELEMENTS OF A TRIAL. There are essentially four parts to a trial: opening statements, the plaintiff or petitioner's case, the defendant or respondent's case, and closing arguments.

Notice that a trial begins with an opening *statement* but ends with a closing *argument*. They are quite different. Argumentative interpretation of what happened in your case is reserved for the conclusion. The beginning of the trial is a chance for your attorney to tell the judge what you intend to prove during the trial. Your attorney will likely give a brief overview of the case and explain her theory of why you should win.

After both sides have given their opening statements, the plaintiff or petitioner will present her version of the facts. The lawyer will call witnesses intended to back up the theory of the case. If the issue is child custody, your lawyer will call witnesses who, for example, are intended to prove that your husband is a bad father. The most important witness in the case will be you.

After being called to the stand, your lawyer will ask you a series of questions. This is called direct examination. You and your attorney should have gone over these questions many times; you should not be caught off guard by a question your attorney asks. Answer the questions directly and honestly.

In cross-examination, the opposing lawyer will attempt to discredit you and your testimony. He will be very aggressive, even hostile. Expect incidents in your past to come up that may cast doubt on your integrity. Also expect facts to come up that contradict what you testified to. Do not expect to be treated with much respect.

There are two important factors that determine how a judge will rule in a case—law and facts. Laws are subject to much interpretation, and each lawyer will, throughout the course of the trial, argue as to why a certain legal interpretation should apply to a certain set of facts. The bulk of the trial will be taken up with what happened during the marriage—the facts of the case. When contradictory facts are introduced, it is up to the judge to decide who is telling the truth and what the real facts are.

After the plaintiff presents her case, the defendant will get a chance to do the same. Witnesses giving a very different interpretation of what happened will be called. Facts about you that are unflattering will come out. Your spouse may very well lie while on the stand.

After all witnesses have been called, closing arguments are made. Although the judge may have made up his mind by this point, these arguments are important. It is a chance for your lawyer to put forth the best interpretation of the facts, as proven with the evidence presented. After both sides have concluded their arguments, the judge will rule on the case. He may also take the matter "under advisement" for determination at a later date.

HOW TO MAKE A GOOD WITNESS. How you behave, not only while testifying but throughout the trial as well, will have a large impact on the outcome of your trial.

Dress nicely. Exercise decorum and self-restraint. Do not overreact. Do not argue with your spouse. Present yourself well. Do not chew gum. Be on time. Do not whisper (pass notes instead). Be respectful.

The key to being believed when testifying is to be honest. Your testimony must be credible, make sense, and have the ring of truth to it. Judges instinctively know when someone is lying. Speak up. Be calm. Do not memorize answers. Listen to the question, and answer only the question asked. If you do not understand a question, ask for it to be repeated. If the opposing lawyer attempts to bully you, do not let him. Do not avoid the truth, even though it may be unflattering. Be clear, concise, and honest, and all should go well.

APPEAL. If either party is unhappy with the verdict, he or she can bring a motion to "vacate the judgment." There must be valid legal grounds (e.g., new evidence) for the motion to be successful. Mere unhappiness with the ruling is insufficient.

If the motion fails, the case can be appealed to a higher court. The appeals court *will not* retry the case, and it will not likely hear any new facts. The appeal must be based on an argument that the trial judge made a mistake as to the law, not in his interpretation of the facts. A legal or procedural mistake that adversely affected the outcome of the trial is what is needed to make an appeal work. And even if that works, the case will be sent back to be tried again correctly. Expect an appeal to be very lengthy and equally expensive.

The Important Legal Concept to Remember: Trials are emotionally difficult and very expensive. If forced to go to trial, make sure to act appropriately and testify honestly. The prohibitive cost of an appeal makes a retrial quite unlikely.

VII

LIFE AFTER
DIVORCE

24

CHANGING PERSONAL RECORDS

Changing personal records
Changing title to property
Changing your name

No one said divorce was easy because it's not. Severing emotional and financial ties, dealing with custody disputes, and rearranging a life are all necessary steps toward a fresh, and hopefully happier, beginning. And, like all beginnings, they start with an ending. Your divorce is final once you get a final divorce decree from the court.

Once that has been issued, there remains some unfinished business that should be attended to, namely, cleaning up personal records and getting a new financial start, alone.

Abby was finally rid of Mitch. Sick of his philandering and irresponsibility, she could hardly wait to buy a new house and get a new life. Throughout her thirty-six years, Abby had consistently paid her bills on time. She was not worried when she agreed to pay for half of the $20,000 in debts that she and Mitch had accrued in their marriage; she was confident that she could pay off the bills. Abby was accordingly shocked when she was turned down for a home loan. It turned out that Mitch did not pay his half of the bills on time, and because they had been married for ten years, much of their credit was joint. Although she knew she was divorced, her creditors did not.

CHANGING PERSONAL RECORDS. Upon obtaining your final decree, the first thing you should do is inform your creditors that you are no longer married. This includes credit card companies, banks, and credit-reporting bureaus. If the final decree dictated that your ex is responsible for any debts, do not count on him or her to let the creditor know. Make sure that you tell them, and make sure that the debt is thereafter reported as your mate's separate responsibility.

You also need to close all joint accounts, if any remain open. If you were given any investment accounts as part of the property settlement, make sure to have them put in your name alone if this has not already been done. This includes stocks, bonds, mutual funds, and savings or checking accounts. If your mate was the beneficiary of your life insurance policy, have it changed. If he was named in your will or living trust (see the companion book, *Ask a Lawyer: Wills and Trusts*), have his name removed. If he is listed on your pension plan, have it modified.

CHANGING TITLE TO PROPERTY. Title to property also needs to be changed if this has not already been done. Your ex-mate's name may be on the title to your car even though it was given to you in the divorce. He needs to sign over his share of the car to you by signing off on the title document to the car. Then go to the Motor Vehicles office and reregister it in your name alone.

If you were given the family residence as part of the settlement, you will need to have your ex sign a deed that transfers his interest in the property to you. This is often done as part of the settlement process—the agreement is not signed until title has been transferred. If this is a task that is still in need of completion, do not attempt to do it alone as a small mistake could cost you hundreds of thousands of dollars. The deed should be drawn up by your attorney. Once you have the deed, have it recorded in the county recorder's office.

CHANGING YOUR NAME. Finally, you may want to change your name. While there are steps one can go through to have this done legally, it is not really necessary. Say you want to go back to using your maiden name. All you really need to do is to notify the appropriate agencies of the intended change—banks, employers, credit card companies, and the local Motor Vehicle Department, to be sure, but, more important, make sure to notify the Social Security Administration. In order to transfer your old Social Security number to your new name, the agency will likely request to see your divorce decree. Finally, also make sure that your passport is in your new name.

The Important Legal Concept to Remember: If you are the only one who knows you are divorced, you may end up getting hurt by the mistakes of your ex-spouse.

25

GETTING CREDIT

Secured credit cards

Auto loans

Passbook loans

If you are fortunate enough to still have good credit at the end of your divorce, count your blessings; many people do not. The problem is twofold. First, bills that were fairly easy to pay with two incomes are more difficult alone. Second, many divorcing people intentionally run up credit cards and otherwise attempt to ruin their spouse's credit as a matter principle, however misguided. As a result, lots of fine folks who always attempted to pay their bills on time find themselves with bills they cannot pay and their credit ruined by the time the divorce is final.

If your credit history has recently turned sour, or if you have never had credit in your own name, fear not. Getting credit is a game; if you know how to play it, you can win. There are three rules to the game. The first rule: if you have good credit, you can get more. The second rule: if you have bad credit, you cannot get any. The last rule: creditors report both good and bad credit to credit-reporting agencies. The trick to winning this game is to manipulate rules one and two to get creditors to give you credit. They will then report you as a good credit risk, even if you had bad credit in the past.

The real key here is rule number three: both good and bad credit are reported to credit-reporting agencies (like TRW).

Creditors use these reports when deciding whether to extend credit. A good report results in good credit, and vice versa. It follows, then, that to win at this game you must get your creditors to report that you are worthy of the risk, which is what credit is. Outlined below are several methods that will enable you to get credit, despite any negative credit history.

SECURED CREDIT CARDS. Most credit cards are unsecured. That means that the credit card company gives the card without any collateral. They trust some people, based on their positive credit history (rule number one), to pay the company the money owed for the goods or services purchased with the card.

A secured card is just the opposite. The credit card companies, based on a negative credit history (rule number two), do not trust other people to pay the money owed. In order to ensure payment, they offer cards that are *secured by some collateral*, specifically, by money. In exchange for a card with, say, a $250 credit limit, the credit card company requires that the applicant open up a bank account in the amount of $250 in its institution. If the cardholder fails to pay the money owed, the security (i.e., the money) will be used to pay the debt.

So, by depositing money in the right bank or financial institution, anyone can get a credit card. An important question to ask potential secured credit card companies is whether the card is reported as secured to the credit-reporting agencies (rule number three). You want a card that is not reported as secured. Why? A secured card that is not reported as secured (and not all are) looks like it is unsecured on your credit report. Other potential creditors who read the report will be more inclined to give you unsecured credit if it *looks* like you have an unsecured card already. You really begin to establish good credit when you have unsecured credit.

Anyone, no matter how bad their credit history, should be able to get a secured credit card. They are offered by most banks, and can also be found in the classified sections of newspapers under "Credit" or "Money to Lend."

AUTO LOANS. Anyone who is trying to (re)establish credit should check out a dealer-financed car loan. The key term to look for is "We carry our own papers." That means that the dealership does not use a bank to finance its used-car loans. Instead, it finances the car itself. If you stop paying, they repossess the car.

The problem with dealer-financed auto loans is the extraordinarily high interest rate one must pay. Whereas most new car loans may hover around 6 percent, a person with bad credit should expect to pay about 20 percent on his loan. By comparison, a $10,000 auto loan with 6 percent interest, if it were to be paid back in three years, would cost $11,800 (6 percent of $10,000 = $600; $600 x 3 years = $1,800; $10,000 + $1,800 = $11,800). The same loan with 20 percent interest, payable in three years, would cost $16,000! If this seems outrageous, that is because it is. However, it also is an opportunity for people with bad credit to both get a car and reestablish themselves financially. Once the loan has been paid back faithfully, it will be far easier to get a loan in the future. Not only will the interest rate be lower the next time, but more dealers will be interested in selling you a car.

One final note about auto loans: an auto loan is a secured loan. The car secures the loan. This is not a negative thing—all car loans are secured.

PASSBOOK LOANS. This method is similar to, but also distinct from, the secured credit card procedure above. The idea is the same—use a savings account to establish credit. It's the execution that differs.

A passbook loan works like this: take a good amount of money—$500, for example—and open up a passbook savings account (a regular savings account) at a bank. Then ask the bank for a loan secured by your passbook savings account. It will give the money to you because the loan is secured by the savings account. Right off the bat you have gotten a major financial institution to give you a loan. That the loan is usually not reported as secured is icing on the cake. Anyone reading your credit report will be far more likely to extend you credit once they see that a conservative institution like a bank was willing to take a risk on you and lend you money.

The Important Legal Concept to Remember: Credit is a game. Once you know the rules, it is not a difficult one to win.

26

VIOLATION AND MODIFICATION

Late child and spousal support
Interference with visitation or custody
When a spouse hides a child
Modification of child and spousal support
Modifying child custody

Another painful reality discovered after divorce may be that you are not rid of your spouse at all. His bad habits and annoying actions are still there to upset you, only once you are divorced, it is almost impossible to get him to change his ways. Even more than a spouse, an ex can vex.

LATE CHILD AND SPOUSAL SUPPORT. Once your divorce is final, the court issues a final judgment, decree, or order (depending upon the state). Both parties are obligated to live up to that decree and follow it in both letter and spirit. When an ex-spouse violates the order, the affected party must let the court know about the violation. Petty violations such as bringing the kids back later than agreed to every Tuesday night, while frustrating, are hardly worth bringing to the attention of the court. Judges have neither the time nor the inclination to deal with such trivialities.

Tardy or even nonexistent support payments, on the other hand, are major violations of the order and should be pursued.

When Jason missed his child support payments for the sixth month in a row, Robin hauled him back to court, and the judge cited him with contempt of court. Not only were Jason's wages garnished in order to pay all back support payments but he was fined $500 as well.

Besides wage garnishment, the court can attach bank accounts, seize property, put a lien against a house, or garnish taxes and Social Security payments in order to get back payments up to date. Because child support arrears are such a big problem now, violators are dealt with harshly. If the spouse who owes the money lives in another state, the Revised Uniform Reciprocal Enforcement of Support Act allows one state to enforce a judgment in a different state, even though the states may have different support laws.

Also, instead of going to court, you can contact the local district attorney. District attorneys of every state are now authorized by law to assist in the collection of past-due child support payments. If the deadbeat parent refuses to cooperate with the district attorney, he could go to jail.

INTERFERENCE WITH VISITATION OR CUSTODY. The right of divorced parents to see their children—to have *frequent and continuing contact* with their own kids—is probably the most protected and the most cherished right they have. Surely the most harmful thing a parent can do to her ex is to interfere with his time with the children. Not only does it harm the other parent, it hurts the children as well.

Interference with visitation or custody is absolutely the single most stupid thing a parent can do. The court will reprimand the perpetrator harshly. Willful violation of the decree by refusing to allow the other parent the time specified in the order constitutes contempt of court. It is a quasi-criminal offense. If found guilty, the parent can be fined, jailed, or both.

Moreover, since *promoting* relationships between the children and the other parent is considered a legal virtue, *interfer-*

ence with that right may constitute a need for a change in custody. For example, if the custodial parent continuously prevents the noncustodial parent from seeing the children, the noncustodial parent would have an excellent chance of modifying the original custody award and getting sole physical custody of the kids (see below). It is the aggressor who ultimately will see less—much, much less—of the children.

If this is happening to you, go see your lawyer. The law is on your side, and you can probably get your ex-spouse to pay the fees and costs you will expend by bringing her back to court.

WHEN A SPOUSE HIDES A CHILD. The most evil thing a parent can do is to move with the children to an undisclosed location. Child abduction is a crime most often perpetrated by *parents*. If your child has been concealed by your former mate, the first thing to do is to contact the police, the local district attorney's office, and your state attorney general's office.

The police can help if you suspect that the children are still in your state. The district attorney and the state attorney general's office can use the national parent locator service to help find your ex-spouse. This service can access records in the FBI, Social Security Administration, Department of Defense, and Veterans Administration, which should aid greatly in finding a missing child. If you have reason to believe that they have been taken out of state or out of the country, the FBI can help.

Private investigators are also a good, albeit expensive, avenue to pursue. Finally, there are many private foundations that prove to be invaluable when attempting to locate missing children. Among these are Child Find of America, located in New Paltz, New York, and the Polly Klass Foundation, located in the San Francisco area.

MODIFICATION OF CHILD AND SPOUSAL SUPPORT. After the divorce is final, only a few aspects of the decree can be modified: child custody (see below) and support, visitation, and spousal support. All other parts, including debt division and property settlements, are not subject to modification.

As a general rule, courts do not like to modify existing orders. Divorce courts relax this rule, recognizing that circumstances change. If the facts as they existed at the time of the final decree change considerably after the divorce has been finalized, then the court will be more inclined to modify the order to meet the changed circumstances.

The change must be significant. If one spouse loses a job, a modification in a support award would be proper. A child who develops a medical condition may require an increase in support payments. An ex-mate's new boyfriend is not a reason to modify a support award.

Not all ex-spouses are enemies. If you and your ex can agree on the modification necessary, you need not even go back to court. A stipulation signed by both parties and offered to the court can modify the existing agreement. If you cannot agree, a motion must be brought before the judge requesting the change and setting forth the factual and legal reasons why the change is necessary.

MODIFYING CHILD CUSTODY. Child custody awards are probably the most difficult part of the divorce decree to change. Not only must it be proved that there has been a change in circumstances but one also must prove that this change is in the best interests of the child. This two-part test (a change in circumstances necessitating a modification that would be in the child's best interests) is a difficult one to pass, to say the least.

The final decree gave joint physical custody of their five-year-old daughter, Sydney, to both Christine and Louis. Three years after the divorce was final, Louis was involved in a car accident, rendering him a paraplegic. After he got out of the hospital, Christine took Louis back to court, requesting sole physical custody of their daughter. She claimed that Louis could no longer care for Sydney as he had previously.

The court denied Christine's request. Although Louis's accident clearly constituted a change in circumstances, the court did not think that his condition made him any less fit a parent; it was in Sydney's best interests to see her dad as much as she had before. Because Sydney was now eight, Louis's condition did not affect his parenting ability.

Had Sydney been two at the time of the accident, the court might have decided otherwise. In that case, it probably would have been in her best interests to live full-time with the parent who could care for her needs.

The Important Legal Concept to Remember: The final decree is usually that—final. Support modifications require a change in circumstances, and custody modifications require that and a finding that the change is in the child's best interests.

PRENUPTIAL AGREEMENTS

After his divorce from Julia was final, Al made a lot of money acting in television commercials. That is where he met Petra, who was also recently divorced. Because his divorce had been so costly, Al was nervous about what would happen to his money if he married Petra. His lawyer suggested a prenuptial agreement. Petra suggested breaking up. Al did not know what to do.

PRENUPTIAL AGREEMENTS IN GENERAL. A prenuptial agreement is also called a premarital agreement. It is an agreement between a couple made prior to their marriage that states what will happen to the property of one or both of the parties should the union fail. And while it undoubtedly has a patina of pessimism about it, it equally undoubtedly creates a promise of protection for the person with many premarital assets.

It is not just the wealthy who may want to utilize prenuptial agreements; they can be of use to almost anyone contemplating marriage. For example, since a prenuptial agreement can be used to indicate who gets what property upon divorce, it may interest any potential newlywed who has been married previously. The high cost of litigation and divorce can be almost entirely eliminated with a well-drafted prenuptial agreement.

A prenuptial agreement is a **contract**. And, like any contract, it creates a set of "laws" between the parties who sign it. It can stay in effect as long as the couple stays married, or it can terminate on the tenth anniversary. It can deal with one main asset, or many small ones. It is up to the couple. A widow may want a prenuptial agreement to state that all property she brings into the marriage from her previous life will remain her sole and separate property, no matter how long the couple stays married or how the property is used. (Separate property sometimes can become marital property if commingled. See Chapter 8, "Marital Property.")

Similarly, a prenuptial agreement can be used to make sure that the inheritance rights of children are protected, that certain debts will be paid, or that alimony will be paid in case of divorce. It can be as broad or as narrow as the circumstances dictate.

To be valid, the agreement must be in writing, both parties must make a *full disclosure* of all assets, and both parties must be *adequately protected* by the agreement. Full disclosure means that both mates have told each other about all of their significant assets and liabilities. Failure to disclose these facts constitutes **fraud**, and fraud invalidates all contracts, prenuptial or otherwise.

Adequate protection means that the agreement is fair and reasonable to both parties. The agreement cannot be so one-sided that it protects one mate at the expense of the other. This does not mean that the agreement must protect each spouse equally; rather, it means that the agreement cannot leave one of the partners impoverished. An agreement stating that all property purchased together will become the property of one spouse would be invalid.

There is one basic limitation on such agreements. A prenuptial agreement cannot contain a provision designed to give up child support in the event of a divorce. The rights of children are independent of the marriage relationship, and neither parent can contract away that responsibility.

CONTENTS OF THE AGREEMENT. A comprehensive prenuptial agreement should probably contain most of the following provisions:

- *A list of all premarital assets:* This would include all real estate, automobiles, personal property, savings accounts, investments, and life insurance.
- *Distribution upon divorce:* The agreement should list how the above-mentioned assets would be distributed should the marriage end in divorce.
- *Distribution of property acquired during marriage:* While it is impossible to list what you will purchase during the course of your marriage, you can set forth general parameters as to how that property will be held and distributed. Will it be joint, or will it be the separate property of each spouse?
- *Appreciation:* If a house brought into the marriage appreciates in value, how will that be accounted for?
- *Debts:* Will marital assets be used to pay off premarital debts of either spouse? Who will be responsible for the bills incurred during the marriage?
- *Investments:* Will stocks, mutual funds, and other investments remain separate, or will they become marital property? Who is the beneficiary of the life insurance, and will that change after marriage?

A valid prenuptial agreement is a two-edged sword. Clearly it circumvents many of the problems that may arise during a divorce. By signing the prenuptial agreement, which declares what is what and whose is whose, the issue of property division is effectively resolved. Many of the costs associated with divorce will have been eliminated. Conversely, by signing a prenuptial agreement, you also agree to **waive** your right to get those items listed in the agreement later. Thus, while any future divorce may be quicker and cheaper, the prenuptial agreement also bars the signatories from getting items they might otherwise have been entitled to had they not signed it.

HOW TO INVALIDATE A PRENUPTIAL AGREEMENT. A mate "stuck" with what he considers to be an unfair prenuptial agreement will have to take the contract to court if he wants it overturned. There are several grounds for throwing out a prenuptial agreement:

- *The agreement is likely to promote divorce:* If the agreement is so one-sided that it would induce one party to get divorced, it would likely be held invalid. For example, an agreement that gives the wife $250,000 if the couple ever divorced might instigate that divorce.
- *The agreement was induced by fraud:* As indicated, if one party failed to disclose a significant asset or debt, then the entire agreement may be void.
- *The agreement is unconscionable:* Unconscionability is a legal phrase used to indicate that the terms of a contract are so unfair, so one-sided, that it would be morally repugnant to uphold it.
- *The agreement was made under duress:* If one party was forced to sign the agreement against his will, the agreement is invalid.
- *The person who made the agreement lacked legal capacity:* An agreement signed while one of the parties was under age, drunk, very ill, or mentally unstable is likely illegal and unenforceable.

The Important Legal Concept to Remember: Prenuptial agreements can protect assets that otherwise may be lost in a divorce. As long as the agreement is entered into honestly, it should be upheld by a court.

GETTING MARRIED AGAIN

Property and money
Stepchildren

Marriage, be it the first, second, or fifth time, is a tricky proposal by any measure. Remarriages, especially, are inherent with the possible pitfalls of stepchildren, ex-husbands, and fear. If you are getting married again after having gone through a divorce, there are some things to know, and some protections that should be taken.

PROPERTY AND MONEY. Much of your divorce was probably spent in the seemingly petty property division process. Having gone through it once, you surely do not want to do so again. There are a few ways to avoid it:

27

- *Prenuptial agreements:* Prenuptial agreements make a lot more sense the second time around. They describe whose property is whose, they keep separate property separate, and they try to settle money issues before such issues arise. (See Chapter 27, "Prenuptial Agreements.")
- *Living trusts:* A living trust is similar to a will, but it allows your estate to pass to your beneficiaries outside probate. A living trust has the added advantage of protecting your assets

from unscrupulous new mates. (See the companion book, *Ask a Lawyer: Wills and Trusts.*)

Know too that any property you received in your divorce settlement is your *separate* property. Just because you remarry, that property does not become joint marital property. The only time your separate property becomes joint property in the new marriage is when it is commingled. For example, assume that you and your new mate move into the house that you had received in the previous divorce. Thereafter, you both pay the mortgage equally for five years. You have commingled your separate property and it is now partially jointly owned.

If you are the spouse who receives alimony, expect it to end once you remarry. Since the point of alimony is to help the less-well-off spouse become reestablished, the money ends upon remarrying as that constitutes becoming reestablished.

If your ex-spouse pays child support and gets married again, do not try to get the support award increased. Even though remarriage is a change of circumstances, the income of a stepparent is usually not considered when determining a modification of child support. And if the receiving spouse remarries, the same applies; a new spouse of the recipient is not a reason for the paying spouse to decrease child support.

STEPCHILDREN. Stepparents have virtually no legal responsibilities for their stepchildren. They are neither obliged by law to support them nor required to pay for their necessities. It is only when the child runs the risk of becoming a ward of the state because of impoverishment that the stepparent may be required to take care of the stepchild's needs. Otherwise, while there certainly may be moral responsibilities to the child, there are no legal ones.

It follows, then, that absent responsibilities, their rights to them are nonexistent as well. A stepparent simply has no rights vis-à-vis her stepchild, for the most part. Without a **power of attorney**, a stepparent cannot authorize medical treatment for her stepchild, and usually has no visitation rights upon divorce. Visitation may be awarded if there has been a close relationship between the two that began while the child was young and continued into the teen years.

A stepparent usually cannot adopt a stepchild. The only time a stepparent can adopt a stepchild is when the biological parent is deceased, the biological parent gives his written consent, or the child has been abandoned by his biological parent.

The Important Legal Concept to Remember: When marrying again, make sure to protect your separate assets. Any new stepchildren are the legal and financial responsibility of their biological parents.

APPENDICES

COMMON QUESTIONS AND ANSWERS

▬▬▬

BEFORE THE DIVORCE

I really can't afford a lawyer. Can I act as my own attorney?
If you must, you must. Acting as your own lawyer is called acting in pro per. In your favor is that judges are more lenient with pro per plaintiffs, and usually give them every chance to make their case. Have no illusions, though, acting in pro per is an uphill battle.

My attorney wants to take my divorce as a contingency case. Is that okay?
No. Divorces cannot be paid on a contingency basis.

Is it possible to get my attorney to reduce his bill?
Yes. It is fine, probably even smart, to challenge a legal bill. Some unscrupulous attorneys bill for time that they did not really put into the case (called padding the bill), while others do not mind reducing the bill a bit if it will keep a client.

My lawyer tells me I have a bad case. Can I fire her? Can she quit?
Sure, you can fire your lawyer. This is your case. Make sure to get your file back—it is your property, and your attorney must return it to you. As for quitting, your attorney can quit, but only if it does not prejudice your case. If it is a week before trial, the answer is no. In some states, the attorney will need to ask permission of the court to get out of the case.

We never married. Do I have any rights?
Possibly. In some states, couples who have been together for some length of time are considered married as a matter of law, even if they never got the "piece of paper." This is called common law marriage. To prove you have a common law marriage you must (1) live in the District of Columbia, Alabama, Colorado, Georgia, Idaho, Iowa, Kansas, Montana, Ohio, Oklahoma, Pennsylvania, Rhode Island, South Carolina, Texas, or Utah; (2) have lived together for a lengthy period of time (it varies, depending upon the state); (3) have presented yourselves to the community as husband and wife; and (4) meet the legal requirements for marriage (e.g., not be a minor, freely consent to the union, be single at the time of the union, etc.).

SEPARATION AND DIVORCE

Is a separation agreement really necessary?
No, not really. The advantage of a separation agreement is that it spells out responsibilities during the gray area between separation and divorce, when financial duties are not defined. On the other hand, obtaining one may take a lot of work and cost a lot of money. The smarter move is to get legally separated so that you would no longer be responsible for each other's post-marital debts.

Does it make a difference whether my divorce is based on fault or no-fault?
Assuming your state allows fault divorce, and not all do, then fault may allow you to get more alimony, property, or child support *if* you can prove that your spouse did something wrong and was indeed at "fault."

PROPERTY

I think my husband has a hidden bank account somewhere. What can I do?

Suspicions, even well-grounded ones, are not enough. You must be able to *prove* that your husband has hidden some money. Proof requires testimony from witnesses, or documents evidencing the fraud.

I live in a community property state, and I make twice as much as my wife. Does she own half of everything we bought even though I paid for most of it, and even though title is in my name alone?
Yes, she does. In a community property state, assets are owned equally by both spouses. Title is irrelevant. If it makes you feel any better, she owns half of the debts too.

I have an interest in my husband's retirement. Do I have to cash it out, or can I just keep it until I retire?
You can keep it, but you will not receive any benefits until your ex-husband retires. By filing a Qualified Domestic Relations Order (a QDRO or Quadro), you can have the plan adminis-trator send you your share of the check upon your husband's retirement. Your share, though, stops growing once you divorce.

My ex-wife refuses to sign the papers transferring the car. What can I do?
There is not much you can do other than taking her back to court. A small consolation is that she probably will end up hav-ing to pay your legal fees and costs.

MONEY

Can I get rid of my support obligations in a bankruptcy?
Basically, no. The Bankruptcy Reform Act of 1994 made it very difficult for people to rid themselves of divorce obligations in a bankruptcy. Check with a bankruptcy attorney to see if any of your particular debts are dischargable, or see the companion book, *Ask a Lawyer: Debt and Bankruptcy*.

How long will I have to pay alimony?
Your divorce decree should have a specified date when your

spousal support will end. If it is indefinite, then you will likely have to pay until your wife dies or remarries, or until there has been a change in circumstances.

I lost my job. Can I just stop paying support until I get another one?
Legally, no. In reality, maybe. Failure to pay support is illegal, and if your ex-spouse takes you back to court, you can end up in a lot of trouble. In practice, it may take a while for your spouse to get you back to court, and you may find a new job in the meantime.

Can my ex-husband and I both claim our daughter as a dependent?
No, you cannot. There is only one exemption per child per year, and it cannot be claimed by both parents.

CHILDREN

He is a terrible father. Can I deny him custody or visitation?
Probably not. Courts rarely deny a parent the right to see his or her child. Supervised visits are a more likely possibility.

She refuses to pay for transporting the kids back and forth. What can I do?
If the final divorce decree mandated that she share the costs, then you need to bring her back to court. If not, there is not much you can do, unless either of you has moved far away recently. In that case, a court might order her to help.

I don't like how my ex-wife is raising my daughter. Can I do anything?
Not unless your daughter is in imminent peril. Courts are not in the business of micromanaging parenting skills. Since you both likely share legal custody, your ex-wife has an equal right to raise your daughter as she sees fit.

Can I stop his girlfriend from being with my kids?
No, unless she is a threat to your children. In that case, it is advisable to get a restraining order against the girlfriend.

Can I move from the state and take the children with me?
If you have physical custody, you should not try to do so without either the permission of the court or the agreement of your
ex-spouse. If you do not have physical custody, taking the children without permission is kidnapping.

ENDING THE CASE

*Is it okay to let my wife's attorney draft the marriage settlement
agreement?*
It may even be a good idea. Someone has to draft it, and if your
wife's attorney drafts it, then she will have to pay for it. That
could easily cost her a few thousand dollars. Once it is written, have your attorney review it to make sure that it accurate-
ly documents what you agreed to.

I am unhappy with the proposed settlement. What can I do?
You can go to trial. If your mate is unwilling to compromise,
you have little choice. And if your spouse sees that you are willing to take the case all the way to trial, that may be enough to
scare him back into negotiations.

I am unhappy with the results of my trial. Can I appeal?
You can, but you probably should not. Appeals are extremely
costly, and rarely successful. The appeals court will not hear
your case anew; it will only look to see if there has been a legal
procedural error, and if there was one, it will send the case back
for a new trial. To appeal successfully, you must win your
appeal *and* your new trial.

AFTER THE DIVORCE

*I was married for twenty years. Do I have to go back to my maiden
name?*
Not at all. You can still use your married name.

Do I really need a prenuptial agreement the second time?
Not unless you want to go through this again.

GLOSSARY

Actuary: A statistician or economist who computes the present value of retirement plans that will pay out in the future.

Annulment: A proceeding brought in divorce court that establishes that a marriage never existed.

Arrears/Arrearages: Money that is overdue and unpaid. The term usually applies to support payments and mortgages.

Associate: A lawyer at a law firm who is merely an employee, not a partner. Associates tend to be younger and less experienced than partners.

Bar Association: An association of lawyers found on local, state, and national levels.

Battery: A crime resulting from conduct that is intended to harm another and does in fact harm that person. Besides a criminal wrong, battery is also a civil offense that can result in an award of money damages.

Best Interests of the Child: The legal standard used to decide who should get custody of children.

Breach: The breaking or violating of a law, right, obligation, duty, or contract.

Brief: A written argument submitted to the court that supports a legal position in a case.

Capital Gains Tax: A provision in the income tax laws providing that profits from the sale of a capital asset are taxed at a certain rate. Profits from the sale of homes and stocks often result in the need to pay a capital gains tax.

Change in Circumstances: The legal standard used by the court to determine whether to modify an existing order.

Child Neglect: Any form of cruelty to a child's physical or emotional well-being caused by neglect.

Collateral: Property that is pledged to secure the payment of a debt. The borrower agrees to give up the property if the debt is not paid.

Commingled Property: Property that came into the marriage as a separate asset, but becomes partially joint marital property due to a commingling of assets and finances by the couple.

Community Property: The name given to marital property when acquired by a couple in one of the community property states. Community property is divided fifty-fifty at divorce.

Complaint: The papers that initiate a lawsuit. A complaint sets forth the parties, the jurisdiction of the court, and the grounds upon which the suit is based, and it requests that the court solve the problem by granting relief.

Contempt of Court: Any act in willful disobedience of a court's authority. Failing to comply with a court order constitutes contempt of court. Contempt of court is criminal in nature.

Contingency Fee: A contingency fee arrangement is one in which the attorney is paid out of any money damages collected in the case. Contingency fees are normally 33 percent of any money received.

Contract: An agreement between two or more parties based upon an offer, acceptance of that offer, and an exchange of money, goods, or services. A contract creates an obligation by the parties to do or not do a certain thing.

Custodial Parent: The parent who is awarded physical custody of children in a divorce.

Default: Failure to answer. When a party who is being sued fails to respond to the complaint, he is in default. A party who defaults may lose the case.

Defendant: The party who is sued.

Deposition: Sworn testimony given before a trial that carries the same weight as testimony given at trial.

Discharge/Discharged: In bankruptcy, the release of the debtor from his legal obligation to repay debts. Once a debt has been discharged, the debtor no longer owes the money to the creditor.

Discovery: The pretrial process of discovering what the other party knows about the facts of the case.

Divorce: The dissolution of a legal marriage.

Divorce Decree: The final court order that rules on the issues in the case and grants the divorce.

Equitable Distribution: A system used by many states that attempts to distribute all property from the marriage equitably and fairly.

Equity: The value of property once all debts have been subtracted from its worth.

Fair Market Value: The amount that a willing buyer would pay a willing seller for a piece of property.

Fault: A wrongful act. A divorce based on fault requires that the plaintiff prove that the other party committed the wrongful act alleged.

Felony: Of the two types of possible crimes—misdemeanor and felony—felony is the more severe, and is punished more harshly.

Fixed Visitation Schedule: In a parenting arrangement after divorce, a schedule that lists the specific times the noncustodial parent will have visitation with her child.

Flat Fee: A payment arrangement wherein the exact fee is set and will not be raised or lowered.

Fraud: A false representation of the truth that is intended to induce another to act or rely upon the falsehood. A fraud may result from lying, omitting the truth, or concealing the truth.

Goodwill: The good name of a business. The favorable consideration given by the public arising from a well-run business.

Joint Custody: A shared custody arrangement, usually, but not always, fifty-fifty.

Judgment: The official and final decision of a court.

Jurisdiction: The power and authority of a court to decide certain cases. It also sometimes refers to the geographical location of a court.

Legal Custody: One of the two types of custody. It is the right of a parent to make important decisions on behalf of his child.

Legal Separation: A court order that sets forth the terms (financial, custodial, etc.) under which a married couple will live separately.

Levy: The legal process whereby property is seized and sold, or money has been attached.

Lien: An encumbrance or claim upon property used to secure payment of a debt. Once the debt is paid, the lien is removed. If the debt is not paid, any sale of the property will first be used to remove the lien and satisfy the debt.

Litigation: The adversarial legal process whereby one party sues another to right an alleged wrong.

Marital Property: Property owned by both spouses, usually referring to property acquired while the couple was married.

Marriage Settlement Agreement: The agreement between a divorcing husband and wife that resolves all or some of the issues in the divorce.

Motion: A request made before a court that asks the court to rule on a matter in a certain way.

Net Income: The actual take-home pay someone receives. It is the amount remaining after deductions have been made from gross income.

Noncustodial Parent: The parent who was not awarded custody and who has visitation rights instead.

No-fault: A system of divorce available in all states that allows one spouse to file for divorce without having to prove that the other spouse did anything wrong.

Paralegal: A person with some knowledge of the law who works under the supervision of an attorney but is not a lawyer.

Party/Parties: The people involved in a lawsuit. Each person is a party to the suit; collectively, all plaintiffs and defendants are the parties.

Personal Property: All property other than real estate.

Petition/Petitioner: In a divorce action, the party who files the petition for divorce.

Physical Custody: One of the two types of child custody. The party granted physical custody is the one with whom the child will primarily reside.

Plaintiff: The person who starts a lawsuit by filing a complaint.

Power of Attorney: A document authorizing one to act on behalf of another legally.

Property Settlement: An agreement made between spouses that divides the marital property. It may be part of a larger agreement.

Qualified Domestic Relations Order: A court order that tells a pension plan administrator how a pension shall be distributed among divorcing spouses.

Real Property: Land, and usually whatever is built on that land.

Reasonable Visitation: An unscheduled visitation arrangement that allows a noncustodial parent time with his child in a reasonable manner.

Response/Respondent: In a divorce, the party responding to the divorce petition.

Retainer: An up-front payment to a lawyer that the lawyer applies to the fees and costs generated in the case.

Seizure: Taking possession of another's property.

Self-help: Taking the law into one's own hands without following legal procedure.

Separate Property: That property owned by a spouse in his or her own right during marriage.

Service/Serving: The delivery of a legal document upon a party.

Sole Custody: A term that usually applies to physical custody when awarded to only one parent.

Sole/Solo Practitioner: An attorney who practices alone, without partners or associates.

Status Quo: The existing state of things at any given date.

Summons: The legal instrument initiating a lawsuit. Delivered to the defendant with a complaint, it notifies the defendant of the suit.

Title: Ownership of property. Usually associated with real estate.

Tort: A civil, as opposed to criminal, wrong that results in personal or property damage.

TRO: A temporary restraining order. It is an emergency order of the court that usually prohibits a person from taking an action. A TRO will be in effect for only a short period of time, until the court can hear the merits of the dispute.

Uncontested Divorce: A divorce in which the respondent never answers the complaint, thereby defaulting. The court will then automatically grant the divorce. It also sometimes refers to a mutually agreed-upon divorce.

Uniform Reciprocal Enforcement of Support Act: A law that provides for enforcement of a child support order issued in one state to be carried out in another state.

Wage Garnishment: A court-ordered method of debt collection whereby the debtor's wages are withheld to pay the debt.

Waive/Waiver: Knowingly giving up some right.

INDEX

M8194–TN
19